BEST PSYCHOLOGY IN FILM

# *BEST PSYCHOLOGY IN FILM*

BEST PSYCHOLOGY IN FILM

*First Edition*

Published in 2018
All Rights Reserved

Copyright © 2018 by Katherine Marshall Woods

Except as permitted under the U.S. Copyright Act of 1976, no part of this publication may be reproduced, stored in or introduced into a retrieval system or information storage, downloaded, transmitted, distributed, reverse engineered or distributed, in any form or by any means including electronic and mechanical recording, scanning, photocopying, currently known or hereafter invented in the absence of permission in writing from the publisher.

To obtain permission, contact:
k.marshallwoods@psychmindedmedia.com
To learn about the author visit: www.psychmindedmedia.com.

ISBN:  978-0-578-42811-6 (hc)/ 978-0-578-42902-1 (pb)/
978-0-578-42811-6 (eb)

# Best Psychology in Film

Katherine Marshall Woods

BEST PSYCHOLOGY IN FILM

BEST PSYCHOLOGY IN FILM

*To Faith*

# BEST PSYCHOLOGY IN FILM

BEST PSYCHOLOGY IN FILM

## *CONTENTS*

| | | | |
|---|---|---|---|
| Acknowledgments | | | 11 |
| Introduction | | | 13 |

### *AND THE NOMINEES ARE……..*

| | | | |
|---|---|---|---|
| I. | *Arrival* | Intrusion | 21 |
| II. | *Fences* | Disappointment/Betrayal/Regret | 33 |
| III. | *Hacksaw Ridge* | Convictions/Perseverance | 65 |
| IV. | *Hell or High Water* | Poverty/Retirement | 89 |
| V. | *Hidden Figures* | Acknowledgment/Defended | 113 |
| VI. | *La La Land* | Emerging Adulthood/Loyalty/Self-Doubt | 133 |
| VII. | *Lion* | Adopting/Integrating/Agape | 161 |
| VIII. | *Manchester by the Sea* | Grief/Bereavement/Coping/Resolved | 193 |
| IX. | *Moonlight* | Identity/Shame/Addiction | 247 |

| | |
|---|---|
| Final Thoughts | 279 |
| References | 283 |
| About The Author | 301 |

## BEST PSYCHOLOGY IN FILM

## *ACKNOWLEDGMENTS*

I would like to thank my Lord for providing me with the Holy Spirit to follow His path. Thank You for providing me the strength to find the means to indulge in my passions. To my parents, who provide unlimited encouragements and support every dream I imagine. To Jay, my muse and husband; my gratitude to you is boundless. Richard, thank you for mentoring me and being a shepherd on my journey. To the former APA's PsycCRITIQUES, Huffington Post, Thrive Global, and Medium platforms that have welcomed me and demonstrated that there is a readership for the following pages. Thank you to my aunt Nadine, who shared with me the joy of authoring. Thank you my sisters: Aisha, Bonita, Ezinna, Jangar, Lisa, Maia, Tanesha, and Tracie who encourage me to follow my love for psychology and film. To Ruby, thank you for your continued support, listening ear, and belief in me, my abilities, and vision. To Cheri and Ryan, thank you for your time and dedication to this project. And to my unwavering supporter, cheerleader, lent ego, and voice of reason when my voice fades—a million thanks to you Pepper.

# BEST PSYCHOLOGY IN FILM

# *INTRODUCTION*

When one's mental health and psychological functioning are posed as a source of discussion, it is not uncommon that anxiety ensues in the listener(s). Such statements are made in "humor" that nothing is wrong, no concern is needed, and the conversation should not be taken seriously. Questions are asked of whether what is said is being analyzed, whether the person should censor what is spoken, and wonders of whether "you can get into my head" loom. Such statements are typically stated with laughter and in jest. Unfortunately, in the United States and around the world, stigmas regarding mental health and psychology remain ever present. According to Seeman (2015), who performed a survey involving one million respondents from 229 territories, he found that stigma related to mental illness and health continues to exist, which contributes to emotional distress "and leads to shame, avoidance of treatment, social isolation and, consequently, a deterioration in health" (p. 309).

In recent years, psychology has become an increasing topic of discussion. There is a global attempt to understand motivations behind behaviors—even atrocities such as mass and school shootings, which may further support negative attitudes of the public regarding mental health (Sartorius, 2007). There has also been a growing interest in gaining new information regarding diagnoses and treatment for conditions, such as post-traumatic stress disorder (PTSD), attention deficit hyperactivity disorder (ADHD), and other illnesses that afflict many. As these are all important and informative aspects of psychology, the field offers a wide breadth of data that is greater than what is covered in media segments when breaking news occurs. In actuality, information yielded from psychology is substantial and certainly beyond what can be offered within the pages of this book. Though, through the use of a familiar medium such as cinema, we are able to explore a myriad of psychological factors that are offered within the art of entertainment.

## Why Cinema?

Cinema is a widely supported source of entertainment globally. In America alone, films gross over eleven billion dollars annually (Box Office Mojo, 2016), where individual films can earn millions of dollars beginning the opening weekend. Films share a diverse set of stories with countless audience members. As a result, this makes film a powerful vehicle that exposes individuals to not only comedy, horror, love stories, and the like, but different ways of life, alternative approaches to manage situations, and varying means to relate to others. Further, what can be found within cinema is a rich depiction of psychological dynamics that live within the scripts and performances that document stories and character's lives.

In the winter months, annually for the past ninety years, individuals have found themselves in exciting times with the presentation of the ACADEMY AWARDS®, commonly known as the "OSCARS®". Currently, news coverage flutters in discussion regarding the movies worthy of nomination of the prestigious Academy of Merit Awards. Interest in whether specific celebrities will be present, and television shows dedicated to commenting upon the best and worst dressed on the red carpet, fill hours of network time. This event that occurs one evening a year by the Academy of Motion Picture Arts and Sciences (A.M.P.A.S.®) provides the public with information regarding the movies of the previous year that were written and directed in a manner noteworthy. This platform also highlights actors who portrayed characters in a fashion that moved audiences. In sum, these films are considered extraordinary among their constituents. Recognition provided by the A.M.P.A.S.® is substantial. In the short term, being nominated for an OSCAR® can further the trajectory of a film to become a mainstream title by influencing the public to take notice and support the work. In the long run, the film, actors, directors, and writers become acclaimed, where the success of both being nominated and awarded an OSCAR® remains noted throughout the duration of careers.

### Psychology and Film?

Psychology is all around us. The field is diverse, where one can easily observe psychological dynamics when directly interacting with others and when engaged in solitary contemplation. Psychological elements can be seen throughout the lifespan, from birth until one's death. In watching characters within movies, psychological concepts are equally present. In fact, specific films such as *12 Years a Slave*, *Lincoln*, and *Apollo 13* for examples have been recognized due to the accuracies in historical facts and life situations that were portrayed. Consequently, films can be fertile tools to explore and apply past psychological theory and remain abreast of new psychological findings within literature.

Partnering with film to examine psychological occurrences also welcomes individuals within such conversations. As mentioned above, stigma regarding mental health and psychology remain a challenge within our communities. Working to better understand psychology in life situations can be beneficial in demystifying the field. In doing so, we can work to actively combat stigma, which can lead to "discrimination in all walks of life, decreasing self-esteem and self-confidence" (Sartorius, 2007, p. 810).

Inviting film, a source of entertainment to many, to illustrate the presence of psychological dynamics creates an environment that provides a comfortable space for individuals to engage intimately with psychological concepts and foster inspiring connections that can be otherwise overlooked. Such concepts when contemplated can cause difficult emotions to arise, evoke memories of the past, and encourage individuals to avoid further thought into uncomfortable ideas. However, film can create an atmosphere that increases one's comfort by enabling the use of a mechanism that helps protect from becoming overwhelmed by challenging thoughts and feelings that surface when exploring emotional experiences. In particular, the defense mechanism of displacement is an integral assisting emotional tool in this process.

Displacement is a "higher-level neurotic defense" (Gabbard, 2005, p. 36), one that is classified as sophisticated, mature, and healthy. Specifically, displacement allows one to redirect "emotion, preoccupation, or behavior from its initial or natural object to another because its original direction is for some reason anxiety ridden" (McWilliams, 2011, p. 139). In action, when one experiences a feeling that poses a threat of discomfort, to resume a comfortable state, one may express the feeling through an alternative vehicle, such as play or a substitute behavior. In this case, film readily lends itself to be an auxiliary mechanism. Uneasy tense situations that cause intolerable emotional discomfort can be witnessed from a distance, through a scene, in the comfort of a seat in a theater or one's home. Characters involved in situations that would typically elicit anxiety, if were real, can be safely viewed with the understanding that the story lacks a personal connection to the viewer. Film provides a contained experience with a known beginning, middle, and ending. As such, when the film has a predetermined ending, the experience does not have to endure for the viewer; rather, the option remains present to pause the film to process the material periodically when needed. Further, considering psychological dynamics within films fosters exploration of psychology in the safety of a script; one that is written to entertain, yet may illuminate novel concepts. Films provide a level of containment that motivates viewers to become inspired and expand their thought in what may be possible in relationships with others, career, love, fantasy, and life.

The partnership between psychology and film is not a novel venture. Psychological writings historically have explored related concepts found within cinema. Additionally, within psychological training, it is not uncommon that students are assigned to view films that depict specific symptoms and diagnoses found within characters. As such, professors tend to use film as a method to demonstrate to students specific themes and dynamics that may occur within the course of treatment. However, expert knowledge in psychology or cinema is not required for curiosity; all are welcomed in the exploration.

### Best Psychology in Film

It is important to note that within each film frame and interaction between characters, psychological factors are at work. This book will review global themes found within OSCAR® nominated films as well as offer case formulations applicable to characters that have been acknowledged during the February 26, 2017 ACADEMY AWARDS® ceremony, honoring films of 2016.

Within the chapters that follow, the OSCAR® nominated and winning films are examined using a psychological lens. Film themes are considered and supported by current research found within the field to reveal specific dynamics in the world around us. Character analyses that provide a summary of character's emotional functioning for recognized roles that earned nominations and awards for "Actor and Actress in a Leading Role" and "Actor and Actress in a Supporting Role" for films that were also nominated for "Best Picture" are explored. These character analyses include an in-depth view of the character's style in navigating the world, emotional conflicts presented, tendency to manage situations and stress, quality of defense mechanisms, feelings (affect), use of emotion and interpersonal capacities. These sections are geared towards understanding an individual's emotional functioning and personality style that assists in capturing the uniqueness of the character's presentation and the impact the character's presence had upon shaping the film.

Upon this journey, it is recommended that viewing the films occur prior to reading each chapter to become familiar with the content. If this is an overzealous notion, possibly the content in this book will entice. It is my hope that, after screening the films and reading this book, one will be exposed to psychology in a manner that is welcoming to those acquainted with the field and spark interest in those who ask the question, "What is psychology about?" As we embark on this discovery, I wish you thoughtful viewing and happy reading.

BEST PSYCHOLOGY IN FILM

*AND THE NOMINEES ARE........*

## BEST PSYCHOLOGY IN FILM

BEST PSYCHOLOGY IN FILM

## *ARRIVAL*

Directed by: Denis Villeneuve

## *SCENE I*

*A view of a lake is followed by a shot of Louise and her baby born at the hospital.*

**LOUISE:** "I used to think this was the beginning of your story. Memory is a strange thing. It doesn't work like I thought it did. When you're so bound by time, by its order."

*Louise leans in close to her baby lovingly. A nurse holds the baby. When the baby cries, dialogue of Louise instructs playfully to the baby to come back to her. Dialogue of Louise and her young daughter is stated as they play in the lawn, lake in the background.*

**LOUISE:** "I remember moments in the middle."

*Dialogue of Louise with her young daughter continues. Her daughter is shown as an adolescent angry with Louise. Her daughter is captured at a doctor's appointment. Louise speaks with a physician and later sobs in the hospital corridor alone.*

**LOUISE:** "And this was the end."

*Louise sniffles asking that her daughter come back to her. Louise walks down the hospital corridor slowly.*

**LOUISE:** "But now I'm not so sure I believe in beginnings and endings."

*Louise walks up a flight of stairs into a classroom.*

**LOUISE:**　　　　"There are days that define your story beyond your life. Like the day they arrived."

# *INTRUSION*

## BEST PSYCHOLOGY IN FILM

*"Vision is the art of seeing things invisible."*

– Jonathan Swift

When under extreme stress, individual's responses may vary. For some, distress can be tolerated for specific lengths of time. For others, the senses can become overwhelmed. In an effort to protect oneself, the person may attempt to emotionally separate from the experience, appear in a state of shock, physically shut down and become unconscious. Once the exposure to the overwhelming stimulus(i) has concluded, one is left to wrestle with their thoughts and feelings. They must struggle to make sense of what they have seen, heard, smelled, touched, and tasted. As the mind attempts to process what it has been exposed to, events can begin to manifest that are atypical to the person's global functioning. At times, what is experienced can begin to interrupt daily functioning and become symptomatic. In particular, symptom criteria found within the trauma-and-stressor-related disorders in the *Diagnostic and Statistical Manual (5$^{th}$ ed.)*, (DSM-5), the domain home to the diagnoses of post-traumatic stress and acute stress disorders, amongst others, can become present. Such symptoms include intrusion, a persistent negative mood, avoidance of stimuli that reminds the individual of the traumatic event and arousal. Within the film *Arrival*—directed by Denis Villeneuve, Louise Banks—acted by Amy Adams, displays changes in her emotional operations following the exposure of aliens whom arrive on earth. Specifically, Louise exhibited behaviors similar to those outlined in diagnostic criteria for the trauma related disorders of acute stress and posttraumatic stress disorders, where she became particularly vulnerable to symptoms of intrusion.

"The experience of a traumatic event is one of the critical events that can give rise to intrusive images" (Boelen & Huntjens, 2008, p. 217). Intrusion, defined as "recurrent, involuntary and intrusive distressing memories" (*DSM–5*; American Psychiatric Association, 2013, p. 280), can emerge after one has been victimized, exposed to combat, natural or human-made disasters, and the sudden onset of a medical condition, for examples. Psychological distress following exposure to a traumatic or stressful event is quite variable. As such, symptoms of trauma, including intrusive symptoms, can manifest in numerous ways. Most commonly, intrusion presents as recurrent images, memories, flashbacks and nightmares. Additionally, it is not uncommon for the clinical picture of an individual to also include a combination of fear, sadness, and externalized anger (*DSM–5*; American Psychiatric Association, 2013). Intrusive symptomatology "may vary by individual but typically involves an anxiety response that includes some form of re-experiencing of or reactivity to the traumatic event" (*DSM–5*; American Psychiatric Association, 2013, p. 282). Thus, individuals who are exposed to trauma describe the experience of intrusive symptoms as feeling one is "[reliving] the event as though it were continually recurring in the present" (Herman, 1992, p. 37).

When one experiences intrusive symptoms, one finds that moments "break(s) spontaneously into consciousness, both as flashbacks during waking states and as traumatic nightmares during sleep" (Herman, 1992, p. 37). These symptoms tend to have the commonality that they are felt as if the emotion or content is similar to the traumatic event. The presence of intrusive images causes physiological reactions that can be brief lasting seconds or occurring over days (*DSM–5*; American Psychiatric Association, 2013). Thus, despite being in a place of safety, within the mind of an individual experiencing intrusive symptoms, the traumatic event is very much alive.

Louise is introduced as a linguist professor employed at a university in Seattle, Washington. On a typical day, the world learns that twelve alien transports have settled in various locations around the world. Not surprisingly, there were numerous unanswered questions and many individuals responded with fear. People believed that the world was vulnerable to an apocalyptic, catastrophic end, and the arrival of the aliens was a sign to perform extreme behaviors, such as mass suicides. When Louise's mother inquired regarding her emotions, Louise asked her anxious mother in a calm manner, "Do I seem nervous?"

As many, Louise remained abreast of the developments related to the arrival of the aliens. Media filmed individuals in a panic, looting in various countries and exhibiting desperation. She saw that, for some, the arrival of the aliens and their mysterious presence was interpreted as a calamitous event where she remained unencumbered; and appeared curious. Her intrigue fueled interest in working directly with the military when officials arrived at her office door requesting her services to interpret the alien's means of communication. Louise lacked hesitation to become involved and believed that her specific expertise would be of benefit to their team.

Upon Louise's arrival to the camp, she observed an individual being medevaced from the secured government grounds. The military's physician, Dr. Kettler—performed by Frank Schorpion—informed her that "not everyone is able to process experiences like this." Dr. Kettler's response suggested that individuals who are exposed to unfamiliar circumstances that bear stress can become overwhelmed. As a result, the senses can fail to be capable to fully integrate what is experienced in a meaningful way. These experiences can cause specific psychological and physiological responses that may cause one to require medical attention, even emergency care.

Preparing to enter the "shell" (the alien's habitat) for the first time, Louise dressed in the required protective gear. She listened to the mathematician on her team, Ian Donnelly—performed by Jeremy Renner—ask questions regarding the alien's presentation in an effort to emotionally prepare for the experience. As the team drove to the shell and embarked on the mechanical lift to enter, Louise's breath remained steady. After entering the alien's habitat, Louise saw the inside of the shell contained a gravity-less environment. In response, she began to struggle comprehending the extraordinary atmosphere. Her breathing transitioned from deep and paced to rapid and shallow. Her eye contact initially attentive to stimuli became unable to fix upon an object and waned. Louise's thought content, which was typically organized and goal-directed, became compromised, where she was unable to create full comprehendible sentence. When encouraged by Colonel Weber, performed by Forest Whitaker, to leave the lift and fully enter the shell, Louise was unable to provide a comprehensive response and mustered, "I think." Rather than allow her to continue to struggle to process what was experienced, Colonel Weber took her by her suit and accompanied her into the shell to meet the foreign beings. Once the aliens presented themselves, Louise responded with saucer-eyes and took a short breath inward. Her physical response marked a sudden surprise by the alien's presentation. This surprise and shock caused her to physically take a step back, to provide space between her and the alien figure.

Following exposure to such novel circumstances, "intrusive imagery is a common response in the aftermath of a stressful or traumatic event" (Verwoerd, et al., 2011, p. 161). "The development of characteristic symptoms" can last from "three days to one month" for acute stress disorder, and additional months thereafter for a diagnosis of posttraumatic stress disorder (*DSM–5*; American Psychiatric Association, 2013). Features such as intrusion can begin immediately thereafter exposure to a traumatic event and worsen after the traumatic exposure. Within these intrusive images, full traumatic events are absent. Rather, partial memories become available for the individual to relive. Presently, "we lack understanding of why only some moments within a trauma are [re]experienced as intrusive memories and how these moments involuntarily return to mind" (Clark, Holmes, Wooldrich & Mackay, 2016, p. 505).

Those who possess intrusive symptomology after a trauma also may have "recurrent distressing dreams in which the content and/or affect of the dreams related to the event(s)" (*DSM–5*; American Psychiatric Association, 2013, p. 281) may occur. After meeting the aliens, Louise began experiencing intrusive images spontaneously. Specifically, she began to encounter visions throughout the day. Images of the aliens intruded her dreams. The nature of Louise's employment fostered an environment where she became preoccupied with the aliens. In particular, the lack of containment her work offered, where conversations consistently centered on the presence of these beings, generated an overwhelming saturation of conscious thought in an effort to understand the alien's means of communication. Boundaries that enable work-life-balance to foster self-care and time to process novel information were absent from Louise's work setting. Her work environment also influenced inadequate rest and sleep, where she commented that her overall functioning was influenced by fatigue and being "overworked." The all-consuming nature of her job to gain answers regarding the aliens was notable within her dream, which depicted an alien piercing her personal boundaries by being located in her bedroom rather than its shell. The combination of intrusive images and distressing dreams rendered Louise, a linguist, unable to articulate her experience to her colleague Ian when he asked, "You alright?" "I'm not sure it's something I can explain," she replied.

It is expected that persons will struggle to describe the nature of intrusion. Symptoms feel real in quality. These thoughts provide partial information of a difficult event to process. Once an intrusive symptom completes, the individual must reorient to the here and now rather than to the time in which the traumatic event occurred. Consequently, at times, the individual must regroup to orient to time, where they physically are (place), to who they are (person), and to what was happening in their environment (situation). Additionally, the individual may have difficulty understanding the content of the intrusion, as it does not provide a full account of their past experience. To those who experience intrusion, symptoms can be overwhelming and can compromise typical functioning. On most occasions, when these symptoms materialized for Louise, they caused her to stop in her tracks and surrender to the images.

Further, intrusive symptoms can also include "dissociative reactions," where one experiences symptoms of depersonalization and derealization. In the event these symptoms occur, the individual can feel detached, "and as if one were an outside observer of one's mental processes or body" (depersonalization) and present with a "persistent or recurrent experience of unreality of surroundings" (derealization) (*DSM–5*; American Psychiatric Association, 2013, p. 272). Within Louise's experience, on one occasion when standing in the military camp, she began to feel that she was floating in a prohibited area of the alien's shell. She noticed the ink in which the aliens used to write was upon her hands. At this moment, her symptoms of intrusion caused her to experience derealization, where she lost awareness of time and the location of her physical body. When derealization occurs, one views object's motion at a slower pace and observes objects "in a daze" (*DSM–5*; American Psychiatric Association, 2013, p. 283), similarly to Louise's experience.

Within the film *Arrival*, it was learned that Louise's intrusive imagery were not events of her past, as found with the presence of intrusive imagery that manifest for those who have experienced trauma. Rather, these symptoms were foreshadowing her future. The quality of Louise's intrusive imagery, which was later identified as being incongruent with the diagnoses of stress and trauma related disorders, albeit were depicted in a manner that captures the expression of intrusion and the impact that these symptoms have on one's life.

As mentioned earlier, trauma symptoms are demonstrated in various ways. Some exposed to trauma will never develop symptoms related to diagnoses within the trauma- and stressor-related disorders. Others will struggle for days, months, even years to create a cohesive, logical narrative to understand and integrate the traumatic event(s) into one's life. Though meeting and working with foreign creatures could elicit a trauma response and symptoms that impede upon one's ability to function, Louise was effectively able to emotionally cope in an adequate manner. Her emotional presentation of experiencing intrusive imagery did not manifest challenges in her ability to perform her work and relate productively with others. With the possession of emotional strengths and resources, she was depicted as one able to prevent the development of a cluster of symptoms that would warrant a diagnosis found within the trauma- and stressor-related diagnoses.

# BEST PSYCHOLOGY IN FILM

BEST PSYCHOLOGY IN FILM

## *FENCES*

Directed by: Denzel Washington

## *SCENE I*

*Sounds of a truck alternated between driving and coming to a stop. Troy and Jim vacillate between standing on the back of a rubbish truck and lifting cans of trash into the vehicle.*

**JIM:** "Troy, you ought to stop that lying." (laughs).

**TROY:** "I ain't lying. The nigga had a watermelon this big, talking 'bout what watermelon Mr. Rand. I like to fell out. What watermelon Mr. Rand? And it sittin' there big as life."

**JIM:** "What Mr. Rand say?"

**TROY:** "He ain't said nothing. He figure if the nigga too dumb to know he's carrying a watermelon, he wasn't gonna get much sense out of him. Trying to hide that great, big, ole' watermelon under his coat. Afraid to let the white man see him carrying it home."

**JIM:** "I'm like you, I ain't got no time for them kinda people."

**TROY:** "Now what he look like gettin' mad cause he seen the man from the union talking to Mr. Rand?"

**JIM:** "He come up to me talking bout 'Troy Maxson gonna get us fired.' I told him, 'Get away from me with that.' He walk away from me calling you a troublemaker. What Mr. Rand say?"

| | |
|---|---|
| **TROY:** | "He ain't said nothing. Told me to go down to the Commissioner's office next Friday. Whoa! They called me down there to see them." |
| **JIM:** | "Well, long as you got your complaint filed, they can't fire yah. That's what one of them white fellas tell me." |
| **TROY:** | "I ain't worried about them firing me. What, they gonna fire me 'cause I asked a question? That's all I did. I went to Mr. Rand and I asked him. I asked him, 'Why? Why you got all the white mens drivin' and the colored lifting?' Told him, 'What's the matter? Don't I count?' Think only white fellas got sense enough to drive a truck? Hell, that ain't no paper job. Anybody can drive a truck. How come you got all whites driving and the colors lifting?' He told me take it to the union. Well, hell, that's what I done. Now they want to come up with this pack of lies?" |
| **JIM:** | "I told Brownie if the man come and ask him any questions, just tell the truth. Ain't nothing but somebody trumped it up on yah 'cause you filed a complaint on." |
| **TROY:** | "Brownie ain't got that much sense. Man wasn't thinking 'bout nothing. All I want them to do is change the job description give everybody a chance to drive the truck, Oi!" |

*Troy thumps the truck alerting the driver to continue on the route.*

| | |
|---|---|
| **TROY:** | "Brownie can't see that. He ain't got that much sense." |

*Troy hits the truck. The truck drives down the street.*

*DISAPPOINTMENT*

> *"It was one of those times you feel a sense of loss,*
> *even though you didn't have something in the first place.*
> *I guess that's what disappointment is—*
> *A sense of loss for something you never had."*
>
> – Deb Caletti, *The Nature of Jade*

Dreams and aspirations are a natural yet risky part of life. When goals are met, positive emotions are had. There is a sense of relief, fulfillment, achievement, and pride. Once celebrations conclude and all resume to normal life, one's thoughts wander to what novel dreams and accomplishments can be made. Similarly, in the darkness of life events, there are pains and sadness felt by experiences that did not yield the believed fruits of labor and desires. Despite persistently sowing, no harvest was reaped for efforts, which leaves past dreams lost. "We are all disappointed in our own way" (Chandler, 2010, p. 604). Bronstein (2015) posited that, "our desires and aspirations are met regularly with nonfulfillment" (p. 1173). These "emotions have a powerful impact on our lives: They shape our behavior" (Marcatto & Ferrante, 2008, p. 87). Negative and painful feelings ensue where we wished "we had made a better decision" (Marcatto & Ferrante, 2008, p. 87). In life, there are "many kinds of [disappointments that] exist for different reasons and with different consequences" that surface from their presence (Chandler, 2010, p. 606). Within the film *Fences*—directed by Denzel Washington—the Maxson family, comprised of husband, wife, and son, experience momentous disappointments that influence the trajectory of their independent and interconnected lives.

"We feel disappointed when we find ourselves wishing that events of the world had turned out better for us" (Marcatto & Ferrante, 2008, p. 87). At times, hopes that one has appear distant. If obtained, luck may be attributed to its attainment. Other times, the opportunity to reach one's goal is in eye's sight, and when not obtained, one questions what can be done to remedy the situation. When the response is that nothing will change the undesired outcome, one wonders what could have been done differently.

As disappointment arises, there becomes a comparison between "'What is' with 'What might have been'" (Marcatto & Ferrante, 2008, p. 87). Bronstein (2015) cited, "I cannot think of any aspect of life that does not involve some sense of disappointment" (p. 1173), normalizing this emotional experience. He continued that,

> The degree and persistence feelings of disappointment can vary greatly: it can fuel and promote development, helping us search for new experiences, new ideas, and new ways of communicating, but it can also become pervasive and hinder progress and emotional development (Bronstein, 2015, p. 1173).

Researchers have found that "feelings of dissatisfaction and disappointment are strongest where the chances for corrective reaction are clearest" (Roese & Summerville, 2005, p. 1274). Members of the Maxson family remained cognizant of the presence of alternative lifestyles; one's that included fame, success, fulfilled marriages, and pursuits of dreams. Yet the influence of societal pressures, family systemic patterns, and individual lifestyle choices negatively impacted the family from embarking upon corrective journeys.

**Husband: Troy Maxson**

Troy Maxson, performed by Denzel Washington, found that his life included disappointments that permeated through his clear and drunken thoughts. He expressed, during many of his tirades, feelings that he had opportunities taken from him due to being an African American man in the 1950s. As a result, Troy could not see that "the world was changing" as Rose, his wife—performed by Viola Davis—noted. For Troy, "the experience of disappointment keeps us grounded and in touch with reality and is central to the development of our capacity to think" (Bronstein, 2015, p. 1174). Instead, when others spoke regarding opportunities for youth, specifically in the realm of sports, Troy's ability to conceptualize a world where African American's were invited, encouraged to play and contribute to professional teams was restricted. As a result, his son's interest in pursuing football to obtain a college education was met with Troy's resistance where he faithfully conveyed, "the white man ain't gonna let him get nowhere with that football. I told him the first time he come to me with it." Despite having "the support of others and the social availability" from his wife and best friend, who shared their knowledge of increased opportunity for those of color and encouraged him to broaden his perspective of the present world, his support system was unsuccessful "in shaping his response to his past experienced disappointments (Chandler, 2010, p. 605).

Troy frequently reminisced on his past. He held fond memories of playing baseball, an activity that brought him the most pride in his life. He attributed this sport to rescuing him from a life a crime, and provided him hope for his future. His accomplishments were extraordinary, possessing batting averages more impressive than the professional baseball players of his time. When it was suggested by his friend, "You just come along too early," in regards to his inability to be accepted into the professional leagues, Troy responded, "There ain't never been a time too early." According to Bronstein (2015), "Disappointment does not just reflect that we are not always able to have what we need and desire; it refers also to not being able to be as good and special as we would like to be" (p. 1174). Being employed to play professional baseball would have been a means for Troy to exhibit and properly showcase his unique talents. In the absence of such appreciation he felt unsuccessful and bereaved that his one effort of dreaming and hoping resulted in, "And what it ever get me? I ain't got a pot to piss in or window to throw it out of."

For Troy, "the experience of feeling disappointed becomes pervasive and ever present rather than temporary" (Bronstein, 2015, p. 1179). His recollection of his past sporting days frequented conversations with all whom held close relationships with him. His lack of success based upon prejudices remained a consistent interloper within the discussions. Because his disappointment was so great, this emotion "form[ed] the basis for judging events and circumstances" that was desired for himself and in which he applied to other's desires despite their relevance (Chandler, 2010, p. 594). Because of his lack of opportunities within the field of sports, he believed no one similar to him in race—specifically an African American male, and certainly his son—would ever have a fair opportunity to achieve success.

"Disappointment stems from the comparison of an actual outcome with a better outcome that might have resulted had world events occurred differently" (Marcatto & Ferrante, 2008, p. 87-88). Bronstein (2015) noted, "as in daily life—we are confronted with disappointment. We have to survive the disappointment that we are not as good as we would like to be" (p. 1174).

Because Troy was unable to pursue his sporting dreams, his feelings of disappointment influenced his global self-esteem, where he responded by feeling dissatisfied with his overall life. "Disappointment might be seen as a subset of 'dissatisfaction'—it certainly involves dissatisfaction and yet one can be dissatisfied without being disappointed" (Chandler, 2010, p. 591). Troy struggled with managing such feelings and realizations. As a consequence, Troy's means of learning to live with disappointment was found in the satisfaction he obtained through establishing an intimate extramarital relationship that brought him joy and peace. Troy described his satisfaction as,

> She give me a different idea. A different understanding about myself. I can step out this house and get from the pressures and the problems be a different man; don't have to worry about how to get the roof fixed or pay the bills or, I can just, be a part of myself I ain't never been before.

He continued,

> I can sit up in the house and laugh. You understand what I'm saying. I can laugh out loud. And it feels good. It reaches all the way down to the bottom of my shoes. I can't give that up.

**Wife: Rose Maxson**

Rose Maxson, performed by Viola Davis, is introduced as a dedicated wife to Troy Maxson. Within this spousal role, she prided herself on being a homemaker, a loving mother, a maternal presence to Troy's eldest son, and a kind companion with his friend. With the smiles and laughs gained by being Troy's wife, Rose equally experienced concerns, fatigue, and sadness. "Disappointment bears a close relationship to both frustration and loss"

(Bronstein, 2015, p. 1175). Rose struggled to bear witness to the chronic disappointments of her loved ones while being able to acknowledge her own personal regret.

As the woman of the home, an attribute she provided to her family included being empathetic to her husband's sorrows. Frequently, she became the individual equipped to assuage relational conflicts found in the relationships held between her husband and his sons and her husband and his brother. These tasks were taxing, where many times Rose possessed little additional patience, tolerance, and emotional strength thereafter. Fully committed, Rose engrossed herself in the world of her husband willingly and consciously. Rose described to her son,

> I didn't know to keep up his strength I had to give up little pieces of mine. I took on his life as mine and mixed up the pieces, so you could hardly tell which was which. It was my choice, my life. And I didn't have to live it like that, but that's what life offered me in a way of being a woman. I took it. I grabbed it with both hands.

In an effort to continue to love and be the wife in which she desired, Rose committed to "stand" with Troy, living in the shadows of his frustration and disappointments with life. In Rose's mind, Troy was "so big. He filled it up. That was my first mistake, not to make him leave some room for me." As a result, though the negative feelings she experienced were heard, her concerns vastly remained unaddressed and censored through the lens of her husband's understanding of the world as unfair. Other times, Rose's concerns were postponed or unspoken of and left in the darkness of her conscientiousness. "For sure disappointments are sometimes set aside, or shelved" (Chandler, 2010, p. 592) where they have an opportunity to aspire for better. In a plea of understanding and empathy, Rose communicated to Troy that she shared the possession of aspirations; ones that had gone unfulfilled, that she too felt immobility and unable to evolve in a progressive manner. She enlightened,

> I got a life too. I've give eighteen years to stand in the same spot with you. Don't you think I ever wanted other things? Don't you think I had dreams and hope? What about my life? What about me?

**Son: Corey Maxson**

Corey, the son of Troy and Rose, an athlete, had the promise of a successful future. He was a motivated student and desired to use his athletic abilities as a vehicle to secure collegiate options. With sport scouts following his performance, he had a final obligation to obtain the permission and signature of his father to permit him to enroll in university with scholarship support. The Maxson family was acutely aware of Corey's talent and that sport would grant him access to a college education. However, due to his father's past failed experiences to play professional baseball, coupled with a strong desire to protect his son from the disappointments of his life, Corey's opportunities were thwarted by his father. As a result, Corey was left to grieve and create alternative arrangements for his future.

Disappointments can arise "when it is set against hopes and expectations that would have it otherwise" (Chandler, 2010, p. 591). Exhibiting an aptitude for athletics in concert with the honor of being recruited, it appeared that Corey's prospects were in order. However, being a minor, he required his parent's agreement to continue to pursue academics, which was a concern for him and his mother. As his father shared great athletic talent in the past, he found having high hopes resulted in disappointment by the lack of opportunities that awaited him. Consequently, due to his father's disillusions, he noted, "I don't want him to be like me. I want him to get as far away from my life as he possibly can get." Corey's father believed that despite his son's talent, playing sports, "It ain't gonna get him nowhere." In response, Corey grew angry and hurt by his father's lack of support.

Corey's disenchantment with his father was depicted in a slow, yet steady manner. Specifically, Corey wished for love to be shown and desired to be "liked" by his father, who clarified to him, "I don't got to like you." Nevertheless, Corey continued to attempt to identify with his father's past accomplishments by engaging in sports, an aspect of his life that brought him and his father joy. Regardless of Corey's efforts, he was met with continued distance from his father. Corey's disappointment regarding the parent/child relationship facilitated frequent conversations with his father that attempted to address dysfunction within their interactions. When Corey did not receive the loving affectionate responses that he craved, his hurt festered. Thereafter, he was no longer able to feel love for his father; rather, he described his feelings towards his father as, "I hate him."

"Disappointment is a sometimes powerful emotion for the individuals concerned" (Chandler, 2010, p. 606). The experience of one or many disappointments can be influential. Specifically, disappointment can be the impetus for changes in one's thinking, interacting, navigating relationships and making life decisions. "An experience might create disappointment that then requires a revision of hopes or expectations and thus a change of values which are then applied in the future" (Chandler, 2010, p. 594). For example, once prohibited from playing sports, Corey's dreams of attending college dissipated. While walking, he became attracted to a poster that advertised career opportunities in the US Military and later enlisted. Though Corey preferred to obtain further education and continue to play sports; due to his father's concerns, firm limits were placed upon him. In turn, Corey experienced personal disappointments of being unable to fulfill his educational and sporting dreams. Thus, Corey was forced to consider alternative solutions for his future that did not require his father's consent and support.

If one were to be honest, there will be times in life where events will not conclude in one's favor, others will not behave in the fashion in which one would hope, and circumstances and personal conflicts may cause hopes to be unfulfilled. "Thus, at least a measure of disappointment is inevitable" (Greenberg, 2015, p. 1218). In response to losing the option of playing a sport to fund a university experience, Corey used his disappointment to "be a powerful source of reflection and of movement" (Chandler, 2010, p. 606). Rather than build his life on sorrows and regrets of yesterday and identify with his father's way of coping with regret, Corey decided to pursue a military career that provided him with a new promise and opportunity for upward mobility.

Given that the Maxson family struggled to manage life's disappointments in numerous ways, it is important to equally highlight that strategies exist in coping and recovering from this specific emotion. When we are willing to invest "ourselves to certain ends and courses of action, we can encounter obstacles and failures that lead to disappointment and a new internal conversation about it" (Chandler, 2010, p. 593). Further, Rose's eloquently emotionally-laden expression of her disappointments related to her life with her husband and Corey's feuding with his father conveyed that sharing one's feelings with one another can be a helpful, even healing process. Wubben et al. (2009) posited, "expressing disappointment to the person that caused this emotion therefore communicates that one had higher expectations of this person" (p. 988). Alerting that one is devastated by feeling let down based upon the actions or inactions of a loved one places the injured in a position of vulnerability that can lead to empowerment. One must be willing to expose hurt feelings directly to the one who has offended and admit to the individual that there is a desire to "establish a mutually beneficial relationship" (Wubben et al., 2009, p. 990). By doing so, the discussion fosters an atmosphere where two people can arrive at a shared understanding and possibly generate a resolution.

Disappointment is a powerful emotion, one that has the ability to haunt someone temporarily or permanently. It is a feeling that has the capacity to free an individual to be capable of conceptualizing a fulfilling life. It "lies in part in its ability to focus our attention on assumptions, hopes and expectations, as well as on blockages, failures and defeats" (Chandler, 2010, p. 590). Communicating with each other the positives that exists in relationships and the sorrow, presents a space for new perspectives to be created. "Disappointment matters" (Chandler, 2010, p. 605). Gaining awareness of each other provides opportunities that "can lead us to try to improve our understanding, to reformulate our theories, and reexamine our assumptions" (Bronstein, 2015, p. 1174) in hopes to build fulfilling relationships in the future.

BEST PSYCHOLOGY IN FILM

## *TROY MAXSON*

Performed by: Denzel Washington

## *REGRET*

> *"You will have to rise up and say,*
> *'I don't care how hard this is,*
> *I don't care how disappointed I am,*
> *I'm not going to let this get the best of me.*
> *I'm moving on with my life."*
>
> – Joel Osteen, *Your Best Life Now: 7 Steps to Living at Your Full Potential*

There are times in life when best-laid plans can go awry. Questions such as *"What could have been done differently?"* and *"Could I have said something else to have changed the situation?"* (Roese & Summerville, 2005) may come about. In an effort to reduce feelings of disappointment and regret, one may take action and attempt to understand their responsibility for the unsuccessful situation. However, in some instances it is learned that "hopes and expectations may be aspirational rather than experienced" (Chandler, 2010, p. 592). In response, individuals can find it difficult to say goodbye to past unfulfilled dreams, which creates feelings of unresolved, chronic regret. According to Joel and colleagues (2012) it is believed that "chronic or excessive regret can be problematic" (p. 348). Regretful experiences can have a tremendous impact on one's personal self, one's family, and social relations alike. Denzel Washington's portrayal of a middle-aged man's struggle within the character Troy Maxson illustrates the impact of regret and how this emotion can shape one's entire world perspective.

"Regret, I began to realize, is delicately and dramatically poised between hope and despair" (Demarco, 2015, p. 55). Munoz-Darde (2016) noted, "in such cases, there is little more to the notion of regret than a preference that the world would be otherwise, and the apprehension that the world is not that way" (p.

780). It "is an unpleasant, counterfactual, self-focused emotion that results from having made an unfavorable choice" (Joel et al., 2012, p. 348). Regret arises "from a comparison between an actual outcome and a better outcome that might have occurred had another option been chosen" (Marcatto & Ferrante, 2008, p. 87). Sadness and hurt ensues, and feelings of disappointment and discomfort remain active. Regret can have a shelf life of a lifetime, where "unalleviated regret is a terrible thing. It is sorrow caused by actions in the past that are beyond one's power to remedy" (Demarco, 2015 p. 56).

When one has dreams that appear within reach, these great opportunities lost "breeds regret" (Roese & Summerville, 2005, p. 1274). The higher the opportunity and greater the cost if failed, the more severe the regret is felt. When one is committed to a specific end and it does not come to fruition, the loss of the dream can feel unfair and the person can feel victimized. Many times, when this occurs, there is a lack of one person to blame; therefore, targets for the pain must be created. Systems and faceless "others" take the fall for barren hopes and dreams. When the person cannot let go and move forward, ruminating on the pain and regret frequents the thoughts of the injured party.

Although Troy found that his sporting efforts did not yield the success he desired, he continued to possess a desire to live in a just world and obtain what he believed he deserved. For example, within his employment, he recognized that individuals did not gain recognition for their tenure as others did based upon race. "Accordingly, regret persists in precisely those situations in which opportunity for positive action remains high" (Roese & Summerville, 2005, p. 1274). Rather than continue to perform the same job duties until his retirement, Troy became motivated to bring his concerns to the union. Though Troy could not turn the hands of time and become a professional athlete, he could fight in this setting for a fair work environment. Munoz-Darde, (2016) noted that, "failure to achieve the end desired is consistent with continuing to strive to get what one wants. So frustrated desire is a kind of pain which can motivate the continued activity of trying to get" (p. 780). As a result of his continued drive to advocate for change, it fostered him to use his regret in a manner to create a world in which he could exert himself and create a difference. Finally, Troy experienced a victory, felt proud of his efforts; and in turn, found a moment of inner peace.

**What Makes This Character Rich?**

"Most people can readily recall or imagine situations in which a poor decision led to painful regret" (Connolly & Zeelenberg, 2002, p. 212). This could not be truer for Troy Maxson. In his recollections of his early life, he reported a history of illegal behavior that caused him to become incarcerated. "That's what I was, I was a robber. I'm gonna tell you the truth. I'm ashamed of it today, but it's the truth." he stated. While incarcerated, he was introduced to baseball, which brought him both happiness and hope to become a professional player following his release. Troy harbored hope that pursuing his passion would lead to a brighter future. Once he learned he would not be a candidate for playing professionally, Troy struggled to be able to effectively process his affect, which made it difficult for him to arrive at a resolution for his conflictual feelings. Individuals can have challenges articulating what they are feeling in particular to feelings of regret. Marcatto & Ferrante (2008) wrote, "it [is] difficult to match the terms 'regret' and 'disappointment' with their own emotional states" (p. 96). For example, Troy begged his wife, Rose, to understand his level of discomfort when acknowledging and admitting to her, "I've been standing in the same place for eighteen years." Troy's inability to make peace with the course of his life caused him to remain emotionally conflicted. In particular, Troy struggled to reconcile his actual life of being married with a son to his idealized fantasized life as a professional athlete.

According to Bronstein (2015), "we come to realize that to a greater or lesser extent we always have to deal with something lacking in ourselves and others, in what we can achieve and what we can obtain" (p. 1174). Despite time moving forward, Troy remained emotionally encumbered and disregarded confrontations that may have helped him become receptive to an alternative interpretation of the life he lived. When concerns were posed, Troy became defensive and frequently used displacement in order to understand his experience. Displacement, a defense mechanism that allows one to possess negative feelings and transfer those emotions onto another party or object, was a frequent tool of Troy's. In particular, "the white man" became an object of negativity rather than considering alternative variables that may have also influenced his ability to obtain employment with professional leagues. Rose asked, "Why can't you just admit that you were too old for the major leagues, for once why don't you just admit that?" The act of displacing negative feelings onto another creates a barrier in being able to consider other reasons that led to negative affect. This is specifically certain when suggesting that a personal attribute or flaw could have negatively influenced the desired outcome. Displacing can become a convenient, effective defense that keeps negative emotions for oneself at bay while an external group or object remains the source of one's existing turmoil.

Troy was aware that if he continued to live his existing life, he would never experience the happiness he desired. "People may regret inactions more than actions in the short run" (Connolly & Zeelenberg, 2002, p. 213), which fostered Troy's motivation to seek pleasure and happiness outside of his life's circumstances. Though Troy could not change the past, he relied upon a second primitive defense, undoing, to create a new life and future for himself. His desires led him to find love with someone who could "give me a different idea, a different understanding of myself," he offered. In this relationship, Troy believed that his mistress perceived him as someone that possessed attributes that made him proud of himself. In creating a new life with a love interest, it allowed him to begin a relationship outside of the shadow of his past regrets and disappointments. The force of undoing was so powerful for Troy that, when confronted by his wife of whether he would continue to participate in his infidelity, Troy remained committed to the relationship despite consequences of developing new future regrets if he continued the affair. "I just can't give it up," he shared with his wife. At long last, Troy found comfort outside of sports and a way to remedy the pain of regret and disappointment. As a result, he believed that the feelings evoked from his affair were worth changing his entire existing world.

One dream lost can have grave ramifications. Such an event can shatter one's hopes, confidence, and self-concept. Certainly, "a dark moment can eclipse a potentially bright future" (Demarco, 2015, p. 57). However, Demarco (2015) suggests that, "there is no point in wallowing in regret" (p. 59). It "might seem pointless: since there is nothing we can do about the past why add suffering to past misfortune by inflicting the pain of regret on ourselves?" (Jones, 2017, p. 416). Regret, being one emotion of many, is a consequence of having choices in life. "Some go well, some go wrong, and those gone wrong spell regret" (Roese & Summerville, 2005, p. 1273). Making choices that serve us well in the present and build the future that we desire is optimum. While making choices, "one cannot avoid regret directly but must avoid the causes that bring it about" (Demarco, 2015, p. 55).

It is impossible to change the past, but we can make decisions that help actualize our hopes and dreams (Demarco, 2015). When regret does surface, we can choose to experience the emotion indefinitely without gains. However, this feeling can be used to be "beneficial for decision making under many circumstances" (Joel et al., 2012, p. 348). It can be recognized that "alternative paths to regret also exist" (Liu & Roloff, 2016, p. 85). We can choose to interface with regret to create positive outcomes, such as hope. We can choose to entertain that there can be "a positive side to regret. It calls our attention to past mistakes and can provide us with a strong incentive to reform" (Demarco, 2015, p. 56). Unfortunately, Troy struggled to accept that "life is always larger than the events that it includes" and "regret can open the door to a better life. This resolve not to repeat past mistakes can gain a victory over regret" (Demarco, 2015, p. 58-56) rather than live a life of emotional suffrage.

BEST PSYCHOLOGY IN FILM

*ROSE MAXSON*

Performed by: Viola Davis

*BETRAYAL*

> *"What irritated me most in the entire situation was the fact that I wasn't feeling humiliated, or annoyed, or even fooled. Betrayal was what I felt, my heart broken..."*
>
> Danika V., The Unchosen Life

"Relationships are hard" is a frequent heard declaration. "Many couples encounter life events with their partners in which they experience specific relational injuries that affect basic trust and result in feelings of anger and sadness that they are unable to resolve" (Greenberg, et al., 2010, p. 28). Two specific events that can cause such injuries in relationships include deception and untruths between two individuals. "Dishonesty causes anger, distress, punitive thoughts" (Rachman, 2010, p. 306) that negatively affect intimate relationships. Specifically, deception and lies that result in "infidelity generates shock, loss, distress, ruminative pre-occupation, self-doubting, lowered self-esteem and anger" (Rachman, 2010, p. 306) within the injured party. When these variables are present, it can be excruciatingly painful, where "even years after the incident has passed, they still harbor bad feelings and no longer feel as connected to, or validated by, their partners" (Greenberg, et al., 2010, p. 28). Rose, performed by Viola Davis, illustrates the effects of infidelity and how it impacts a once trusting marital relationship.

When one commits infidelity, there is a breach in faithfulness. One transgression can break trust due to the person's act of disloyalty to the union. When this occurs, one can feel betrayed by their spouse. According to Rachman (2010), "betrayal is a sense of being harmed by the intentional actions, or omissions, of a person who was assumed to be a trusted and loyal friend, relative, partner, colleague or companion" (p. 304). Research suggests, "betrayals are not uncommon and in some instances have a catastrophic effect on the victim and psychopathological problems emerge" (Rachman, 2010, p. 304). Despite their frequency within interpersonal relationships, "many betrayals are unexpected events that come as a surprising shock; not infrequently, the betrayal is disbelieved at first" (Rachman, 2010, p. 304).

Once one processes the assault of betrayal, it often causes "seemingly irreparable damage to close relationships" (Johnson et al., 2001, p. 145). In part, "the injurious events remain as a symbol of all that is wrong with the relationship and now define relationship safety and trust" (Greenberg, et al., 2010, p. 29). In response, the injured may attempt to assess the emotional safety of the relationship. For example, when Rose learns of her husband's infidelity, she asked, "What I want to know is, what I want to know, is do you plan to continue seeing her? That's all you can say to me." When she was informed that he planned to continue the relationship, Rose's facial response and deflated body posture suggested in that moment her pain grew more severe. "When the other partner then fails to respond in a reparative, reassured manner, or when the injured spouse cannot accept such reassurances, the injury is compounded" (Johnson et al., 2001, p. 145-146). In response, Rose placed an invisible wall between her and her husband that resulted in her ceasing communication with him. The trust in the relationship "is commonly replaced by a barrier and that too, tends to be permanent. Occasionally exceptions occur when the betrayed person acquires new information that disconfirms his/her construal of what happened" (Rachman, 2010, p. 305). For Rose, she was assured by her husband of his intentions to further erode the connection in their marriage, which did not allow her to modify her response to being betrayed. "When partners feel abandoned or invalidated, their trust in their partners' reliability and supportiveness is shattered, they feel betrayed, and this has a deleterious effect on the relationship bond and leaves partners with unresolved hurt and anger" (Greenberg, et al., 2010, p. 28).

Arriving at a resolution is possible once infidelity occurs within a marriage. Greenberg, et al. (2010) reported that, "resolution requires an understanding by the perpetrator of the wrong done and an apology" (Greenberg, et al., 2010, p. 29). Though Troy communicated to Rose his view of the infidelity, he did not offer an apology for his behaviors. Rather, he attempted to help her understand what motivated him to engage in the affair and what made the affair important for continued investment. "Humans have evolved to realize the wisdom of forgiving under some circumstances but not forgiving under others" (Luchies, et al., 2010, p. 734). Due to a lack of an apology and a commitment from her husband that he would discontinue his transgressions, Rose became increasingly defensive and could not forgive his indiscretions. "As the couple experiences failure in their attempts to move beyond such injuries and to repair the bond between them, their despair and alienation deepen" (Johnson et al., 2001, p. 146). For instance, during times of emotional hardships, Rose found that even within these times, her offered support was unwelcomed, which pushed her farther away from her husband. Thus, "mending emotional wounds, restoring trust, and repairing the relationship bond" (Greenberg, et al., 2010, p. 30) was thwarted within her marriage.

Rachman (2010) astutely stated that, "betrayal is a significant psychological phenomenon" that "causes a breach in an existing bond of trust that is usually irreversible" (p. 310, 304-305). Further, "the effects of a betrayal tend to be widespread and lasting" (Rachman, 2010, p. 306). These injured relationships experience a wound that struggles to heal. "The defining feature of these couples is that the injured partner cannot forget the incident nor get over the hurt and anger from the injury" (Greenberg, et al., 2010, p. 28-29). Consequently, "the effects of a betrayal tend to be long-lasting, even permanent, and are well-remembered" (Rachman, 2010, p. 304), leaving the injured party hurt, requiring recovery, and possibly forever bruised.

**What Makes This Character Rich?**

Throughout the film, Rose is found possessing numerous negative emotional responses that are generated from her marriage. Rose, a dedicated wife and mother, functioned as an individual inclined to care for the needs of others rather than her own. Specifically, many times, when individuals were upset and frustrated, she offered support, contained their experience, and helped ease their upset feelings. As a result of attending to others, many times, her personal emotional needs were unrecognized and unmet. In part, Rose consistently presented as a defended individual; one not inclined to share and instead withheld her feelings. As a result of her well-entrenched restricted defensive style, her relationship with her husband lacked the intimacy needed for him to be familiar with her internal experience.

Merriam Webster defines withholding as "to hold back from action, to refrain from granting, giving or allowing" (2017). Withholding one's feelings within relationships has many consequences. On one hand, withholding can have its positive influence on the partnership. Refusing to share negative feelings can allow challenging times and hurt feelings to be minimized where space is created for the individuals to return to positive affect and move forward.

However, the benefits of not sharing such feelings with one's partner tend to be brief, where positive results are immediate and are unlikely to sustain over time. For example, many times Rose was observed hearing her husband's tirades and witnessing moments where her son hungered to be affirmed and validated by his father. When Rose frequently overheard her husband's inability to provide emotional support to her son and could hear his chronic complaints regarding his global dismay her patience grew less. Yet, she never showed others her worn emotional state. Instead of adding to the negativity by sharing her emotional experience, Rose withheld her similar feelings. In doing so, it allowed her to escape fixating on her negative feelings while freeing her to care for others.

On the other hand, "withholding may also have negative relational and affective implications over time" (Liu and Roloff, 2016, p. 73). Being unable or unwilling to share one's authentic emotions with one's partner causes the withholding party to feel unseen, unable to be understood and taken into consideration. When feelings are not addressed, the person is perceived as being consistently capable of coping with any hardships that come their way. Because one presents as stable, even during challenging times, individuals surrounding them may not consider that the person has unmet emotional needs. In part, the person's genuine emotional experience is not expressed, which makes it difficult for others to empathize and connect when they require support.

Further, when feelings are not readily shared, the behavior(s) that are bothersome are more likely to repeat because others are unaware of what is frustrating. "Prolonged avoidance could increase the frequency of the irritant to unacceptable levels, and its importance may increase" (Liu & Roloff, 2016, p. 74). Withholding how one feels after being irritated several times by a similar behavior requires restraint and emotional energy. Rose learned that "as an irritant becomes more frequent and important, complaint withholding may become more stressful to enact" (Liu & Roloff, 2016, p. 74). When her husband entered the kitchen and attributed his brother's military injury to their ability to financially afford the family home, Rose addressed her husband's concerns by noting the positive behaviors he demonstrated towards his brother. When her husband wished to share his frustrations and felt unheard, the interaction upset him. In response, he left the home frustrated and guilt-ridden. Rather than express her feelings of how his emotional experience felt to her, she inquired regarding his anticipated whereabouts. "Where you going?" she asked.

After leaving the home, Rose found herself emotionally drained. She sat at the kitchen table and placed her forehead in her fist, demonstrating fatigue by her husband's constant disappointment with life and his circumstances. "As frequency of irritant and intense emotional reactions increase, greater effort is required to control emotional reactions" (Liu & Roloff, 2016, p. 75). Consequently, when one arrives at the end of their rope and an event occurs that pushes the person or creates pain, negative emotions that are held are expressed in the same manner as boiling water overflows from a pot on a stove. "These injuries often are specific events that only serve to crystalize more general" (Greenberg, et al., 2010, p. 29) problematic dynamics within the relationship.

Despite the energy required to withhold negative emotion, Rose continued to hold her emotional experience internally. As time progressed, Rose's agitation heightened due to her husband's frequent complaints; and eventually she began to share her irritation with her husband. She asked, "Troy what is wrong with you this morning? Don't nothing set right with you. Go on back in there and go to bed, get up on the other side."

Troy responded, "Why something got to be wrong with me? I ain't said nothing wrong with me."

Rose replied,

> Well, you got something to say about everything. First, it's the numbers, then it's the way the man runs his restaurant, then you then got on Corey. What's it gonna be next? Take a look up there and see if the weather suits you.

Rose's first confrontation is significant. Within this interaction she comments regarding her observations yet neglects to share her feelings regarding what transpired. Given one can assume that she felt annoyed and frustrated, due to her omissions, Rose continued to withhold her internal emotional state from her husband that could have further facilitated the conversation. Not until hurt by learning of her husband's infidelity did that experience help enable Rose to become capable of communicating her feelings to him. At this time, Rose's emotions came to a boil, which fostered her to express her painful emotions. She stated,

> I took all my feelings, my wants, and needs and dreams and buried them inside you. I planted a seed and watched and prayed over them; I planted myself inside you and waited to bloom. It didn't take me no eighteen years to realize the soil was hard and rocky and wasn't ever going to bloom.

Rose's pattern of relying upon withholding continued throughout the duration of her character. Once hurt, she silenced herself, where her husband stated, "You ain't want to talk to me in months." Further, Lui & Roloff (2016) found an additional consequence to withholding, where individuals who withhold their complaints for a prolonged period of time of six months to years are more likely to experience regret. In turn, Rose's continued withholding pattern made her vulnerable to become similar to her husband: regretful.

Withholding within an intimate relationship can have varying consequences. Immediately, withholding may serve an individual well where it appears to be an adaptive defense. By doing so, the relationship avoids addressing the irritant and the negative feelings that arise from such exploration. This avoidance places the relationship in a place to resume positive feelings. However, "prolonged withholding is dysfunctional" (Liu & Roloff, 2016, p. 73). Using this defense as a long-term solution encourages problems to be brushed under the rug, and challenges in the relationship will lack resolution. The individuals who withhold "may find it emotionally distressing to withhold their complaints about any frequently enacted irritant regardless of its importance" (Liu & Roloff, 2016, p. 85) and can begin to experience emotional fatigue, a lack of patience, and regret. Rose found this defense mechanism useful within her daily interactions with her family, yet experienced the unpleasant consequences of not sharing her feelings more readily. "Life's pain and difficulties are necessary to arouse the best in us and to fit our life with meaning" (Demarco, 2015, p. 60). Similarly, Rose surprisingly found that as a result of her husband's infidelity, which resulted in the birth of a child, led to an opportunity to experience greater love in her life and satisfy once silenced unmet maternal desires.

BEST PSYCHOLOGY IN FILM

## *HACKSAW RIDGE*

*Directed by: Mel Gibson*

## *SCENE I*

*Narrated while depicting a montage of soldiers in battle, injured men, men on fire, fallen men.*

**DESMOND:** "Have you not heard? The Lord is the everlasting God, the Creator of the ends of the earth. He will not grow tired or weary. And His understanding no one can fathom. He gives strength to the weary, and increases the power of the weak. Even youths grow tired and weary and young men stumble and fall. But those who hope in the Lord will renew their strength. They will soar on the wings like eagles. They will run and not grow weary. They will walk and not be faint."

(Isaiah 40:28, version unknown)

**SOLDIER:** "Desmond, hang on! Hang on Desmond! We're gonna get you outta here!"

*Desmond is carried by multiple soldiers on a stretcher bleeding from his leg.*

# *CONVICTIONS*

> *"The conscientious objector is a revolutionary. On deciding to disobey the law he sacrifices his personal interests to the most important cause of working for the betterment of society."*
> –Albert Einstein

"Morality refers to notions of right and wrong" (Skitka & Mullen, 2002, p. 36). When an individual is placed in a predicament that challenges the core of what is "right" according to their beliefs, a display of conviction, "an unshakable belief in something" (Skitka & Mullen, 2002, p. 36) to illustrate the contribution the belief has upon their character may follow. "Convictions 'go deep' in the individual and influence the way in which she sees the world around her, how she understands herself, and how she organizes and acts upon her other beliefs, aims and projects" (Pianalto, 2011, p. 382). Importantly, "regardless of whether they are through careful reasoning or a moral 'gut level' reaction, moral convictions are nonnegotiable, terminal and fundamental psychological truths" (Skitka & Mullen, 2002, p. 36). Remaining steadfast to one's beliefs is challenging when in an environment that demands performing activities that oppose the morals one holds. While remaining committed, declining participation in requested activities can result in misunderstandings with others, intolerance, impatience, social isolation, and worse, danger. Desmond Doss, "Private Doss," performed by Andrew Garfield in the film *Hacksaw Ridge*, produced by Mel Gibson, illustrates the effects that moral convictions can have upon an individual, and surrounding others, who hold steady moral convictions in a professional environment that demands performing conflictual actions. In the case of the true story of Desmond Doss, his narrative outlined in *Hacksaw Ridge*, depicts specific dynamics that occurred while he served in the US military during World War II.

"Convictions tend to be settled, firmly held and believed to track moral truth, and thus are not primary candidates for revision" as they are held with the belief of "subjective certainty" (Pianalto, 2011, p. 382). Further, they are "the result of a careful, deliberate, and thoughtful appraisal and subsequent acceptance of a specific moral precept" and require no "reason or evidence" (Skitka & Mullen, 2002, p. 36). Convictions provide the possessing individual with a personal level of comfort despite volatile environments and conflicts that can arise with others. Further, convictions grant the individual with "reasonably adequate frameworks for understanding and acting within one's environment, thereby reducing uncertainty and minimizing the experience of error" (Inzlicht, et al., 2009, p. 386). When peers and/or authorities challenge one's convictions, "the strength of belief" (Pianalto, 2011, p. 382) can become stronger and increasingly fixed. In part, "one of the most important ways that attitudes rooted in moral conviction theoretically differ from other attitudes is that people perceive their moral beliefs to be objectively and universally true" (Skitka & Morgan, 2014, p. 99).

Within *Hacksaw Ridge*, Desmond held the commitment that he could not use or touch a gun. For Desmond, his conviction originated from personal past experiences with violence. For example, within his youth, Desmond and his brother were found fighting in the yard by his father. Though his mother encouraged the boys to discontinue their behaviors and solicited the assistance of their father, they continued to hit one another. On the ground tussling, Desmond obtained a nearby brick and purposefully hit his brother on the head. His alarmed parents carried his unconscious brother into the home and tended to him. Desmond, anxious that he had caused irreparable injury, walked with wide eyes and examined a framed posting of the Lord's Prayer and Ten Commandments mounted upon a wall in his home. There he read, "Sixth Commandment Thou shall not kill." After his mother informed Desmond that his brother would recover, he admitted, "I could have killed him." Desmond's mother, a religious woman offered, "Yes, you could have. Murder is the worst sin of all. And to take another man's life is the most egregious sin in the Word itself. Nothing hurts His heart so much." At that time, Desmond's understanding of the consequences of violence that terminates life began to be shaped from this experience and was framed within this religious belief.

Additionally, throughout childhood, Desmond was exposed to domestic violence that occurred in his home. During adolescence, Desmond protected his mother from his father's drunken assaults. One evening Desmond heard his parents fighting and found himself in the position of brandishing a pistol in his father's face in a threatening manner to stop the abuse. During this event, Desmond's father in a stupor requested that he "pull the trigger." As a result of this experience, Desmond attested that he had killed his father "in my mind." With this symbolic kill, it solidified a promise that he would make with God, to never handle a gun again, transforming his belief into a religious moral conviction.

According to Inzlicht et al. (2009) "religion provides standards for behavior by specifying appropriate and inappropriate actions" (p. 386). Religious convictions also offer "buffers against anxiety by providing relief from the experience of uncertainty and error" (Inzlicht, et al., 2009, p. 385). Inzlicht et al. found within their 2009 study that religion acts as a way to suppress reactions to the unknown, which can in turn reduce feelings of distress. The possession of a religious moral conviction defensively may serve a person well preparing for the experience of war. A newly enlisted private, unfamiliar with battle, may question what the experience of war will be like, will basic needs be met, and will one even survive. During this exploration, they learn that uncertainty consistently looms. Owning certitude in one's beliefs may provide comfort to the solider with staunch morals.

Because Desmond's convictions inhibited him from being able to comply with the demands of his job as a solider, he was referred to as a conscientious objector. "The conscientious objecting solider does not perform treason or sabotage, but surrenders himself to incarceration" if necessary to hold his moral convictions (Breakey, 2016, p. 620). Remaining firm in his beliefs, "the solider only withdraws his own contribution, rather than attacking the war effort itself" (Breakey, 2016, p. 620). For Desmond, he supported other's right and willingness to be armed; yet, when asked to conform with the demands of the position as a private, he remained committed that he could not perform the same duty to kill that he understood and respected others would perform. One who has conviction and integrity may lack universality within their thought processes. The individual is adamant regarding their beliefs and their limited behaviors, but does not condemn others for possessing varying thoughts and beliefs. Therefore, there is no judgment and denouncement of others' behaviors and no desire to generalize their convictions onto others to conform (Hill, 2016).

In military training and similarly within the civilian terrain, "we live in asocial world, and public peace and cooperation depend on respecting rules that others have a hand in creating—even if we ourselves strenuously oppose those rules" (Breakey, 2016, p. 618). When a solider conscientiously objects to the requirements of his position, those around him can have numerous reactions. One manner in which peers and authority may respond is with a lack of understanding of one's choice to enlist in the military. When Desmond and his peers were issued their semiautomatic weapon, Desmond shared his moral beliefs with Sergeant Howell (performed by Vince Vaughn) and his peers. "I'm sorry, Sergeant, I can't touch a gun," he informed. As a result, Captain Glover, acted by Sam Worthington, asked, "You're a conscientious objector and you joined the Army?" Desmond responded, "No, sir, I'm a conscientious cooperator." When asked to clarify, Desmond confirmed that he does not kill. Once learning this information, Captain Glover desired to have Desmond discontinue his service, believing that he was a liability to the unit and a lack of an asset to accomplish their missions. Rather than provide support to Desmond and freely allow him to pursue building skills as a medic, as he desired, Captain Glover urged him to conform or to terminate.

"People typically conform to the majority when faced with the choice to accept or reject the majority position" (Skitka & Morgan, 2014, p. 102). Additionally, conformity may occur "to gain acceptance from others" (Skitka & Morgan, 2014, p. 102). When placed under pressure, one may conform once feeling "broken" from the force to comply. When one is tired of the fight and fatigued from being questioned whether their beliefs are incorrect or "right" for the group, an individual is likely to acquiesce.

Further, authority creates motivation for subordinates to conform to standards of procedure. When subordinates cannot follow standards based upon their beliefs, individualistic thought and moral convictions can be perceived as a threat. In the eyes of others, there is danger in engaging in moralism, as individuals view one who will not sway from their strong moral commitments as potentially treacherous. In our society, "integrity looks dangerous" (Breakey, 2016, p. 613). It "requires having rational reasons for one's views, and holding confidence in these views", while having "a commitment to a collective, intersubjective reflective process" (Breakey, 2016, p. 622-623). However, historically exhibiting integrity based upon moral convictions "has also been associated with a disregard for procedural protections and due process" (Skitka & Mullen, 2002, p. 38). Others fear that the individual may evince "empowerment, egoism, personal calling, extremism, investment and unilateralism" (Breakey, 2016, p. 617) that can foster one to think and behave in a manner that is rigid and self-directed. Others fear that one who holds strong convictions will only consider what is "right" for them and how it supports their perspective rather than equally possess consideration for the benefits and rights of others. It is believed that this person can become fixated in the pursuit of one's own self-interest and unable to conceptualize variation or modification to their perspective (i.e. extremist, terrorist, etc.) Individuals with unfaltering beliefs may behave using radical actions to communicate their perspective that can compromise the ability to navigate successfully as a part of the collective society. Further, the individual's level of commitment to their beliefs generates an "unyielding" (Breakey, 2016, p. 617) approach to other's requests and demands.

Though Desmond did not wish to behave in an outwardly defiant manner and was actively engaged in being a part of his peer's unit, he remained noncompliant with the military's rules to remain authentic and devoted to his convictions. According to Desmond, his desire to save people during war would be a benefit for all who were involved. Captain Glover lacked interest in Desmond's motivations. He was unconcerned regarding the reasons why he possessed his belief and lacked concern that "moral convictions can be proactive responses that reflect people's desire to achieve a better world" (Skitka & Wisneski, 2011, p. 329). Rather, he concerned himself with how this specific belief would impact Desmond's ability to follow his orders and how it would negatively impact his job performance as a soldier, "if you can't do it here, I can't trust you to do it (shoot a gun) in battle." As a result, he ordered that Desmond undergo the administration of a psychological assessment to diagnose him with "insanity" which would lead to a Section 8 discharge, deeming him mentally unstable. This diagnosis would ultimately terminate Desmond from the military.

For some, "people are more intolerant of divergent attitudes when they involve issues generally viewed as moral issues" (Wright, Cullum & Schwab, 2008, p. 1461). However, globally "individuals with divergent attitudes about moral issues may be treated differently" (Wright, Cullum & Schwab, 2008, p. 1463). Research suggest that "people do not want to work with, live near, or even shop at a store owned by someone who does not share their moral opinions" (Skitka & Morgan, 2014, p. 103). Sargent Howell announced to his unit that,

> Private Doss does not believe in violence, he does not practice violence. He will not even deign to touch a weapon. You see, Private Doss is a conscientious objector, so I plead with you. Do not look to him to save you on the battlefield; because he will undoubtedly be too busy wrestling with his conscience to assist.

Desmond continued to receive fair treatment from his peers initially. Despite Sergeant Howell insinuated that others should not rely upon Desmond while in battle, individuals within his unit were indifferent to his belief. Sergeant

Howell added, "even if Private Doss' beliefs may cause women and children to die." He continued that the soldiers should provide Desmond with "the full measure of the respect that he is due, for the short time that he will be with us," anticipating that thereafter the soldiers in the unit would begin to challenge Desmond.

Indeed, one peer, (Smitty Ryker, performed by Luke Bracey), began to bully Desmond due to his restrictions. Initially, Desmond's peers supported him, asking that Smitty discontinue the harassment. Thereafter, Desmond tolerated Smitty taking his Bible and examining a picture of his girlfriend inside of the pages. Smitty confronted Desmond regarding why he would not fight, asked whether he believed he was "better than everyone else", and smacked Desmond on the face to determine how he would respond if he were "attacked." When Smitty provided Desmond the opportunity to "take a poke" and hit him in his face, Desmond's peers encouraged that he hit Smitty in retaliation. Smitty, during his confrontation with Desmond shared the sentiments of Ives (2009) that suggest "in some instances a belief in God that leads to reliance on Him for one's moral decision making leads to a form of moral cowardice" (p. 64). Smitty agreed and noted that Desmond's unwillingness to fight, even in the face of being attacked was "cowardice, plain and simple." Still, Desmond's convictions did not waver. "Moral conviction not only inoculates people from authority influence but from peer influence as well" (Skitka & Morgan, 2014, p. 102).

Desmond was determined by the military's mental health provider as "sane". Thereafter, Sergeant Howell suggested that there may exist an approach that could be used where Desmond would discontinue his enlistment voluntarily. Captain Glover affirmed and ordered the creation of a tumultuous environment where Desmond would likely respond by initiating his termination. He ordered, "You restrict him to the barracks and KP. He throws God on you, you throw hell right on him."

Evidently, a person's moral conviction can significantly impact the nature of one's interpersonal relationships with authorities and one's peers. Socially, "moral conviction not only insulates people from peer influence from those who disagree, it also leads people to avoid attitudinally dissimilar others altogether" (Skitka & Morgan, 2014, p. 103). Desmond began to worry regarding how his beliefs shaped the training experience of his peers as Sergeant Howell began to solicit the assistance of Desmond's cohort to provide pressure upon him to comply. Specifically, he created an undesirable environment for the entire unit as a result of Desmond's lack of conformity. Sergeant Howell also attempted several strategies, supported by Captain Glover, to encourage Desmond to end his employment. Initially, he made trainings difficult for Desmond and noted his area was a "pig's sty" despite its immaculate presentation. He encouraged Desmond's peers to consider that "the unit is no better than its weakest member" while identifying Desmond as that individual. Additionally, Sergeant Howell restricted all men to the barracks and required all members to perform KP and take long hiking trips. He provided the unit collective consequences due to Desmond's inability to comply with the requirements of the military. When the unit became exposed to communal repercussions, Desmond's peer level of tolerance and support for him drastically dissipated. For example, as Sergeant Howell increased requirements that were no longer exclusively directed toward Desmond, it enabled the unit to become equally vulnerable to receive indiscriminate illiberal reprimands. Consequently, Desmond was no longer the person to experience arbitrary punitive consequences independently. As a result of this shift, Desmond's peers became invested in reducing the negative experience the unit endured. From Desmond's authority perspective, these methods geared to make him feel unwelcomed were a success. Holding the entire unit responsible would apply pressure from both authority and his peers to urge Desmond to decide to discontinue from the Army freely.

An additional strategy utilized included evoking fear. It was made clear that Desmond's conviction may cause each soldier in the unit harm if he did not have a weapon to protect himself and others. This could be interpreted as: Desmond's conviction can cause each soldier his or her life. Training for war and being told that a peer's convictions could decrease safety can generate "heightened emotional states [that] can exacerbate people's responses" (Wright, Cullum & Schwab, 2008, p. 1463). Once learning that conversing with Desmond was unsuccessful in moving him to comply, coupled with feeling the brunt of Sergeant Howell's severe treatment, his peer's frustrations grew, resulting in physical retaliation towards him.

Similarly to Desmond's commitment to his moral convictions, he was equally committed to his peers in his unit. Upon Sergeant Howell's arrival into the soldier's barracks, he observed Desmond's blood-soiled pillowcase and bed and asked regarding Desmond's whereabouts. Desmond walked into Sergeant Howell's presence and presented with a bruised body and displayed a bloodied face. Concerned for Desmond, Captain Howell empathetically stated, "It's okay, Doss, there is no shame in this," providing him permission to discontinue his employment in the military and ending the savage treatment he received. In an effort to remain in compliance with code, Sergeant Howell commanded that Desmond identify the men who "attacked" him. Desmond reported that he could not identify the men, illustrating for his unit that he remained unified and loyal to them. Consequently, when Sergeant Howell demanded that he reveal who assaulted him, Desmond continued to demonstrate his loyalty by clarifying, "I never said I was attacked." By protecting his peers' identity, Desmond was capable of successfully calming his unit's anxieties and negative feelings.

However, though he was able to regain cohesion with his unit, his lack of compliance to handle arms remained problematic for those in authority.

> When one holds a moral conviction, the person must think deeply about moral issues, and decide on his or her own terms what is right and what is wrong. He or she must then take responsibility for the moral convictions that they have formed by being willing and able to defend them as their own (Ives, 2009, p. 65).

As a result, Desmond was placed in a predicament where he was required to defend his beliefs and face a court-martial. During this time, he was threatened to "spend the duration of the war in a military prison." His continued devotion resulted in detainment and court proceedings where he noted that he felt "like my values are under attack." Given that his direct superiors and peers were unable to persuade him of altering his behavior, his fiancée, Dorothy (acted by Teresa Palmer), in desperation for his freedom begged Desmond, "just pick up the stupid gun and wave it around. You don't have to use it, just meet them halfway." The strength of Desmond's morals proved to be convictions as he explained to her, "but I don't know how I'm gonna live with myself if I don't stay true to what I believe, much less how you could live with me." Rather than free himself by complying and continue to advance his training as a soldier and medic, Desmond was court martialed, while embracing his sustained moral position.

"Studies have suggested that having a moral basis to one's attitude is a strength indicator akin to having more knowledge, or accessibility, or certainty" (Luttrell, Petty, Brinol & Wagner, 2016, p.83). People tend to believe that "a person can decide almost instantly that some political practice he or she heard about a couple of minutes ago, like a bloody war in a distant country or researchers using stem cells, is just wrong" (Bloom, 2013, p. 954). Individuals can impulsively respond to information and generate conclusions; yet these ideas may not endure or generate the strength of a conviction that has the power to influence their personal and others' lives. When an individual expresses a moral conviction, people anticipate that the person will relinquish their belief in the service of avoiding conflict, for conformity sake and to reduce pressures that other's may place on them to change. Others expect "the fact that people are inconsistent in their moral judgments over time...[which is] a mark of insincerity" (Hill, 2016, p. 681). However, one who holds conviction tends to earn the respect of others when they exhibit reflection of their views, can engage in discourse with others pertaining to their and other's beliefs and a humility that fosters reflection and discourse (Pianalto, 2011).

For Desmond, his respect as a soldier was earned upon the battlefield of Hacksaw Ridge. Smitty noted, "I got you very wrong." Captain Glover who articulated earlier, "I want him gone," also requested amends, noting,

> All I saw was a skinny kid. I didn't know who you were. You done more than any other man could have done in the service of his country. I have never been more wrong about someone in my life. I hope one day you could forgive me.

Saving seventy-five lives of wounded Americans, its allies, and adversaries, proved that Desmond's efforts as a soldier without the use of a weapon was in fact an asset to the US Army.

BEST PSYCHOLOGY IN FILM

## *DESMOND PRIVATE DOSS*

Performed by: Andrew Garfield

BEST PSYCHOLOGY IN FILM

*PERSEVERANCE*

## BEST PSYCHOLOGY IN FILM

*"Don't allow your mind to tell your heart what to do.
The mind gives up easily."*
– Paulo Coelho

*"Conviction is worthless unless it is converted into conduct."*
– Thomas Carlyle

When a country is at war, there are some individuals who are required to serve. For others, they have an internal calling to enlist when they see others fighting for their rights and freedom. However, having the desire to join the military when the country is in need can pose personal conflicts for individuals. These conflicts arise when one has a direct incompatibility between what the individual person believes and what is required of them from others. Such conflicts can cause significant interruptions and challenges for the person and for those around them. For Private Desmond Doss, his desires to serve within the US Army caused his unit and superiors to modify their conceptualization of a skilled soldier.

Desmond presented as an individual who had the desire to mend. Once fighting with his brother and injuring him with a brick, Desmond became aware that he could be an aggressor. Fearful of the consequences that could arise, Desmond adopted a Christian perspective to inhibit his participation in future violent episodes.

Within Desmond's adolescent years, he found himself in a protective role, safeguarding his mother from his physically abusive father. During these years, he was also introduced to the power of assisting the injured. As he cleaned windows in his family's church, he heard the makings of an accident. Desmond instinctually responded by running to the scene to be of aid. He found a similar-aged peer providing mechanical services injured by a vehicle that fell upon his leg, tearing an artery. Desmond watched the blood from his wound and quickly began to triage care. He requested that someone provide a pick-up truck for transport to the local hospital as he placed a tourniquet around his leg, stopping the bleeding. Once they arrived to the hospital, the physician inquired who applied the tourniquet to the injured leg and commented, "You might have saved this boy's life." In that moment, time slowed for Desmond. Surveying the hospital and watching medical staff engaged in routine medical duties, Desmond became inspired to heal.

In 1941, after the attack on Pearl Harbor, Desmond noted that, "I took it personally." Thereafter, he witnessed individuals eager to enlist in the Army. He also empathized with the disappointment of those who did not meet criteria for the military; and how many responded by ending their life. For Desmond, "It just wouldn't be right" to not serve. This belief placed him in an emotional and moral conflict. On the one hand, it would not be right to decline serving in the war; and, on the other hand, enlisting in the military would require him to handle a firearm, a requirement in direct opposition to his beliefs.

When enlisting, Desmond was cognizant that his moral conviction of being unable to handle a weapon was counterintuitive to joining the military. In order to ensure that his beliefs would be respected, he requested to be trained as a medic. Being skilled as a medic professional would afford him the opportunity to become trained in medicine, a passion of his and serve the United States efforts. Despite being in war, Desmond's goal was to avoid committing a religious sin; coupled with, "I figure I will be saving people, not killing them." Consequently, the acceptance he had of his personal moral conviction to reframe from using weaponry provided him a lack of felt emotional conflict. Specifically, he felt little discomfort or stress based upon this decision, as it provided him with a solid foundation of certainty.

Initially, Desmond believed that he would be able to maintain his moral convictions with little challenge. He mentioned that he arranged with his enlisting officer to be able to enter battle unarmed and become trained as a medic. His father, a former soldier, warned Desmond that he was attempting to "think it all out" believing that "this war is just gonna fit in with you, your ideas." He suggested that holding his convictions would place him in a position to be disobedient of orders. Desmond noted that he was not blind to the fact that upholding his convictions would be difficult, "I don't doubt that it's gonna be hard." His father assured him that it would be "impossible" to do so. If needed, Desmond was prepared to communicate his beliefs to authority to safeguard his moral conviction. Regardless to his father's precautions, Desmond remained hopeful that the calm and peace that he ascertained from his convictions would be understood and respected; or, at the very least, tolerated by those around him.

### What Makes This Character Rich?

Desmond's anticipated plan to navigate his military experience as a medic provided him with a sense of comfort and control. What he "figured" for himself included saving lives during war and being exempt from handling arms, was in fact an idealized ideation. Further, denial facilitated his feelings of confidence, as he believed that his medic training would commence immediately and the requirements of basic training that involved weaponry training would not apply to him.

Denial, the avoidance "of aspects of external reality that are difficult to face by disregarding sensory data" (Gabbard, 2005, p. 36) fostered Desmond to remain emotionally comforted by his decision to become a medic as a method to evade the requirements of all soldiers: the ability to use a firearm. One could consider that Desmond was young and inexperienced with military procedures. Yet, despite his father's forewarning, a former soldier, Desmond remained optimistic that his beliefs would be respected. He anticipated that his military training coupled with his moral beliefs would not make for an "easy" experience. Desmond confirmed with his father that he understood his concerns while remaining confident that he would be able to successfully manage the challenges he might face by authority and his peers.

Despite the difficulties that Desmond experienced in training that comprised of dejection and encouragement to discontinue, he personally persevered. Though his personal fortitude enabled him to complete basic training and pursue the medic position required great emotional and psychological strength, Desmond's performance upon the battlefield was equally, if not more astounding.

Relying upon his faith, Desmond performed extraordinary actions, and ran into the chaos of battle to save others. Sacrificing his safety, he was able to carry the lives of seventy-five men to asylum due to his persistence and commitment. Desmond was able to actualize his desire to save others while others killed. During the stress of battle, Desmond utilized sophisticated defense mechanisms that made him successful in being able to be a savior to the injured living. In particular, Desmond utilized altruism, anticipation, and isolation of affect.

Desmond consistently displayed altruism, the act of "committing oneself to the needs of others over and above one's needs" (Gabbard, 2005, p. 37). Each time he risked his life in an effort to "just get one more" soldier. In addition, Desmond possessed a significant level of anticipation that allowed him to delay his safety "by planning and thinking about future achievements and accomplishments" (Gabbard, 2005, p. 37). For Desmond, his future fulfillment did not include medals or recognition; he was motivated by the achievement of saving another's life. Lastly, Desmond's isolation of affect served him well during this time. As Desmond relied upon the direction provided by his higher power to guide his behaviors, he also isolated his affect of fear, concern, and desire to survive in order to rescue his comrades. According to Gabbard (2005) isolation of affect allows one to separate "an idea from its associated affect state to avoid difficult feelings" (p. 36). Within the film, Desmond's desire to serve God had the strength to mitigate emotions that might hinder one from being capable of being of service.

The actions of Desmond Doss were undoubtedly extraordinary. Equally striking was his use of "higher order defenses" (Gabbard, 2005, p. 36) during a time of high stress. Ordinarily, individuals display higher functioning in both behaviors and coping strategies when in an environment that poses as safe and comfortable. At these times, individuals are better able to access their personal strengths. Customarily, when under tremendous stress, individuals struggle to grasp the use of sophisticated strategies to operate their environment and regress. As stress compromises emotional and psychological functioning, individuals are more likely able to solicit primitive defenses to be able to manage such situations. This strategy enables the distressed to solicit the least emotional resources necessary to navigate the situation effectively. Of interest, Desmond practices primitive defenses initially, and demonstrates emotional maturity in his ability to use increased complex defenses when under immense stress.

In 1945, Desmond became the first conscientious objector to earn the Medal of Honor, America's highest award for courage under fire. His performance upon Hacksaw Ridge was demonstrative of emotional strength attributed to faith, trust, and loyalty. These attributes resulted in remarkable bravery and courage, saved the lives of many men and infused hope in Desmond's unit by helping the men to advance and conquer Hacksaw Ridge.

BEST PSYCHOLOGY IN FILM

## *HELL OR HIGH WATER*

Directed by: David Mackenzie

## *SCENE I*

*In a small town, a car passes. A blue car drives on a parallel street from where the first car parked. A woman exits the parked car and begins to smoke a cigarette. "3 Tours in Iraq but no bailout for people like us" is displayed on a white cement wall. The blue car slowly pulls up to the side of Texas Midland Bank. The woman walks to the back of the bank, puts out her cigarette and walks to the front towards a church. She places a key into the bank's door and her head is quickly pulled back. She is met by two men, faces masked wearing black hoodies and a gun is pointed at the back of her head.*

*(ELSIE GROANS)*

**TANNER:** "Quiet. Open the door, open the door."

**ELSIE:** "What?" *(GASPING)*

*Tanner hits Elsie against a glass door while entering the bank. Tanner pushes her to the ground.*

*(ELSIE GROANS)*

**ELSIE:** "What in the devil?"

**TOBY:** "Can you please stand up and take us to the cash drawer, ma'am?"

**ELSIE:** "I will not."

*Tanner walks towards Elsie and picks her from the floor, holds her by her head and places the gun to the back of her head.*

**TANNER:** "We ain't asking."

*Tanner helps Elise from the ground.*

**ELSIE:** "There's no money in the drawers yet. It's in the safe and I ain't got the code."

**TANNER:** "Prove it. Drawer!"

**ELISE:** *(GASPING)* "Here."

**TANNER:** "Open the drawer."

**ELSIE:** "I need the keys."

**TANNER:** "Keys!"

*Toby provides Elise keys and throws a bag on the desk. Elise works to open the drawer.*

**TANNER:** "Step back! Damn it!"

*Tanner hits an item in upset after finding the drawer empty.*

**ELSIE:** "Y'all are new at this, I'm guessing."

**TANNER:** "Where's the money?"

**ELSIE:** "I told you, it's in the safe."

**TANNER:** "Well, who has the code?"

**ELSIE:** "Mr. Clauson. He'll be here soon and I suggest you fellas don't be. All you're guilty of right now is being stupid. Just leave and that all it'll be."

*Tanner walks towards Elsie, motions for her to come close and leans in.*

**TANNER:** "Tell me I'm stupid again."

*Toby looks concerned.*

**TOBY:** "What time does Mr. Clauson get here? Ma'am, look at me. What time does Mr. Clauson get here, huh?"

**ELSIE:** "8:30 every morning."

*Elsie whimpers. Tanner takes Elsie by the back of the head.*

**TANNER:** "We're walking. And sit!"

*Elsie hunches while walking towards a chair in the waiting area.*

**TANNER:** "Where do you think your going? Sit on the floor!"

*Tanner cocks his gun and places it to Elise's head. She looks at the gun and he walks away. He turns and looks at Elsie.*

**TANNER:** "You're stupid."

*Mr. Clauson exits his car and walks from the lot to the bank. Elsie continues to whimper sitting on the floor. Tanner and Toby hide behind a wall unseen by the glass door.*

**TANNER:** "This ain't about you, darling."

**MR. CLAUSON:** "Elsie, you all right?"

*Tanner and Toby hold their guns towards Mr. Clauson's face.*

**MR. CLAUSON:** "Good morning."

*Tanner strikes Mr. Clauson in the nose resulting in him falling back. Elsie gasps.*

*POVERTY*

*"3 Tours in Iraq*
*But No Bailout*
*For People Like Us."*
– Hell or High Water, Scene 1

As the world changes, what was once reliable to secure financial stability can change. For ranchers in Texas, shifts in demand for goods and facing natural disasters that causes one to gather life's belongings can alter the landscape of a family's wellbeing. Finding that available resources are scarce and accessing external resources that yield profits are limited, neighbors learn that "there's no one to call around here…these boys are on their own," as stated by Marcus Hamilton, performed by Jeff Bridges in the film *Hell or High Water*. Losing major sources of income brings about significant financial transitions that impact individuals and families psychologically. Once years progress and poverty persists, generations are found living with chronic scarcity. Hope begins to fail and desperation grows. The focus becomes solely to make ends meet. Within the film *Hell or High Water*, Tanner and Toby Howard (acted by Ben Foster and Chris Pine) illustrate the struggle experienced when attempting to manage poverty in the face of losing the family's remains; their land.

Financial strains are not all that uncommon here in the US and worldwide. It is a condition that "can be found in all the geographic regions of the world, all ethnic groups and persons of all ages" (Palomar Lever, et al., 2005, p. 375). Specifically, "the Chronic Poverty Report (2008-9) estimates that 320-443 million people live trapped in chronic poverty: that is, these people remain poor for much or all of their lives and their children are likely to inherit their poverty as well" (Dalton, et al., 2014, p. 165). In the United States alone, in 2017, the poverty level for the forty-eight contiguous states and The District of Columbia ranged from an annual household income of $12,060 for a single occupant household to $41,320 for a household of eight (US Department of Health and Human Services, 2017). For individuals who occupy rural areas in the United States, "poverty seems to be neither a temporary nor a permanent state for many rural, low-income families in the US who move in and out of poverty repeatedly" based upon the vacillation between abundance and dearth of goods (Mammen, et al., 2015, p. 434). Yet the impetus of poverty is variable, and the etiology of impoverished conditions varies greatly per individuals and families.

For many families, poverty comes about due to a change in circumstance. This change, referred to a trigger event, is described within research as events that "occur in all families, regardless of income, and some events which alter lives significantly are beyond the control of families" (Mammen, et al., 2015, p. 446). Mammen and colleagues posited that these events could be "both positive and negative" (2015, p. 446) and change the landscape of a family's financial existence due to specific causes. When positive, the

> events can improve the family economic wellbeing; in the case of low-income families, however, such improvement may occur at a slower rate or the families are less able to capitalize on them because poor families start at a lower resource level (Mammen, et al., 2015, p. 446).

As such, researchers have found that "children from poor families will tend to be less upwardly mobile than children from working-class and middle-class families" (Sakamoto, et al, 2014, p. 196). However, when the trigger event is negative, "these have a far more devastating impact on low-income families because such families typically do not have sufficient extra, or surplus, resources to weather the event" (Mammen, et al., 2015, p. 446). For the Howard brothers, it is described that their entire lives were plagued with poverty. Ordinarily found, "health issues and relationship changes seem to be significant trigger events in the economic functioning of the rural low-income families" (Mammen, et al, 2015, p. 447). For some families, when faced with caring for a dying mother for three months, where "at the end it was pretty rough," can be a significant financial burden on the family, even a trigger event that would change the family's financial terrain. Poverty likely "occurs when a trigger event causes a family's circumstances to change, resulting in a move from one state of economic functioning to another, ultimately, causing a shift in the family's economic trajectory" (Mammen, et al., 2015, p. 445). Though Tanner noted that he could have done something if his mother had asked him, at least, "feed those skinny cows," his brother clarified, "we had nothing to feed them," reminding him that, for the Howard family, the event of their mother becoming ill and ultimately dying was one of many trigger events that resulted in furthering their state of poverty.

For other families, "environmental factors such as a person's family background, the norms of the community in which he lives and the opportunities available, economic or otherwise do matter" (Dalton, et al, 2014, p. 171). Within the Howard brothers' family, interpersonal relationships were historically conflictual. Tanner articulated that he believed that his mother "always hated me for standing up to him" (referring to his father). The children "were all punished" according to Toby. These environmental factors influence a number of mental functions that are directly impacted and diminished based upon the quality of the circumstance. In particular, these functions include decision-making, productivity, and utility (Dalton, et al., 2014). Being raised in a household and exposed to domestic violence and abuse impacts one's ability to be receptive to opportunities to develop specific skills that can lead to success. Experiencing poverty in addition to trauma "leads to a psychology of scarcity that reduces the competitiveness of low-income persons in school and on the job" (Sakamoto, et al, 2014, p. 208) that can foster upward financial mobility. Further, the stressors of poverty and trauma lends family members to become psychologically and emotionally fatigued, whether victimized or whether they are able to remain out of physical harm's way.

When a person is "mentally taxed," the ability to use "slow, effortful, deliberate" thought is a challenge, whereas "intuitive, automatic and effortless" functions continue to thrive (Schilbach, et al., 2016). Tanner's automatic response to the abuse that he experienced from his father resulted in him enacting the role of identifying with the aggressor, where he reacted to his father's assaults with similar violence. According to Toby, Tanner did not learn that "fighting back made the beating last longer." Tanner offered his brother a correction to his understanding and stated, "That's why I stopped fighting and shot that son of a bitch." While Tanner was incarcerated, which added an additional challenge onto the family, the family's global impoverished circumstances continued to descend.

Those who live with shortage have many needs. These demands result in the direct obtainment of tangible outcomes that determine whether one will have shelter, food, and other necessary goods on a daily basis. These responsibilities are most commonly referred to as stressors. For instance, "the poor must manage sporadic income, juggle expenses, and make difficult trade-offs. Even when the poor are not actually making financial decisions, these preoccupations can be distracting" (Schilbach, et al., 2016, p. 438). Because when one is in poverty, by definition they are in a state where one "lacks a usual or socially acceptable amount of money or material possessions" (Merriam-Webster, 2017); obtaining basic needs can be a constant cognitive and emotional exercise. "When you are poor, economic challenges are more than just economic, they are also cognitive" (Schilbach, et al., 2016, p. 438).

Cognitive functioning refers to intellectual processes by which one perceives, becomes aware of, or comprehends ideas. "Many studies in psychology investigate the cognitive and motivational effects of being poor" (Sakamoto, et al, 2014, p. 199). "It involves all aspects of perception, thinking, reasoning and remembering" (Mosby, 2009). Historically, "we traditionally viewed cognitive capacity as fixed, but in fact it can change with circumstances" (Schilbach, et al., 2016, p. 437). Specifically, under constant stress "preoccupations with pressing budgetary concerns leave fewer cognitive resources available to guide choice and action" (Mani, et al 2017, p. 1). Individuals who are exposed to impoverished circumstances can spend the majority of their waking hours contemplating how one will access basic needs for the day and/or maintain the resources that they possess. As a result of focusing upon daily conditions and what is required for immediate survival, "many of these studies often describe poor people as having a present-time orientation, being fatalistic about future events, and lacking in cognitive attentiveness" (Sakamoto, et al, 2014, p. 207). Further, mental processes can become dampened, thoughts can present in an unclear manner, and individuals may experience greater levels of impulsivity where attention is difficult to sustain (Schilbach, et al., 2016). Overall, individuals who experience poverty, "encounter higher stress which interferes with cognitive development and retards the proclivity for a greater attention span" (Sakamoto, et al, 2014, p. 206). Additionally, having difficulty accessing primary resources in itself can have its own negative consequences. For instance, situations where one has "too little food may also affect mental function: thoughts may become lethargic, attention difficulty to sustain, and temptations harder to resist" (Schilbach, et al., 2016, p. 437). Thus, being exposed to poverty has consequences that exceed beyond the ability to spend and have basic needs gratified; poverty can negatively impact one's global cognitive functioning.

Once one has experienced financial stressors long-term, it can be difficult to cognitively conceptualize a life in the absence of such financial challenges. "People born into poverty or oppression don't get a shot at working toward anything other than staying alive" (Kalb, 2017, p. 49). Consequently, one's range of dreaming and aspiring for more and a life in the absence of these demands can feel impossible and unfruitful, given the need to resolve very real immediate, problems. Dalton and colleagues posited that, "failure to aspire may be a consequence of poverty, rather than its cause" (2014, p. 179). They further noted that it is likely that indeed with "other things equal, the poor have to make a greater effort than the rich to achieve the same level of final wealth" (2014, p. 166), but "it is possible to break a poverty trap by altering aspirations alone" (2014, p. 167).

When the Howard brothers' mother died, the family's land was willed to Toby's sons. A dilapidated home, lacking cattle; the ranch was an unwelcoming shelter to a family. Toby informed his ex-wife, (Debbie Howard, performed by Marin Ireland),

**TOBY:** "Momma died."
**DEBBIE:** "When?"

**TOBY:** "A few weeks ago."

After inquiring regarding his emotional wellbeing, she asked, "I guess you be selling the ranch?" Toby notified her that "it goes to the boys." Despite inheriting land, and an estate to raise her children, she responded, "Great, something else I got to take care of."

"Poverty is a life condition that directly affects individuals' subjective wellbeing, but also indirectly promotes the presence of attitudes and behaviors that have a significant impact on their subjective wellbeing" (Palomar Lever, et al., 2005, p. 401). Toby's wife had difficulty conceptualizing the benefits of owning land and a home. She lacked the ability to dream of what the land and home could be and saw it for only how it was in its present state. As a result, due to the repairs the property required and the lack of funds that it generated, she viewed being responsible for the ranch until her sons were able to care for the property as another responsibility that would require her care and attention. When resources are unavailable, being poor does not only equate to "having less money to buy things, but it also means having to spend more" emotional energy to manage life's circumstances (Schilbach, et al., 2016, p. 438). Debbie responded to the information regarding the inheritance by expressing her feelings of being emotionally taxed, and providing a deep sigh to further emphasize her burden. The stressors that are experienced by poverty influence one's perceptions of situations and decisions, which impact one's overall emotional functioning.

Emotionally, "stress is generally understood as the emotional state resulting from a particular relationship between the individual and the environment and produced when the latter is assessed by the individual to be threatening or to endanger his/her security" (Palomar Lever, et al., 2005, p. 378). As one experiences persistent poverty and struggle to create an environment that is profitable, additional concerns arise that,

> if the persistently poor do not have the capabilities to improve their position, they may well remain persistently poor, affecting future generations as well since they are less able to give their children a good start into adulthood in terms of health, education and employability (Mammen, et al., 2015, p. 448).

According to Mammen and colleagues, "it is likely that those families who were already at the bottom of the economic ladder will be further marginalized" (2015, p. 435). Poverty becomes, as Toby Howard described eloquently, "I've been poor all my life. Two of my parents, their parents before them. It's like a disease. Passing from generation to generation. Becomes a sickness, that's what it is. Affects every person you know." The understanding becomes that "the end result may be the creation of the conditions for a permanent underclass that falls into spells of poverty more often, each time less able to reverse the situation for themselves and their children" (Mammen, et al., 2015, p. 435). When one's environment does not lend itself to abundance or to adequate supply, the individual experiences chronic stressors that are generated directly from the relationship that is experienced between the person and their environment. Marcus Hamilton's character relaxed on a porch with his partner, Alberto, performed by Gil Birmingham, and demanded he "Enjoy this little town." Alberto questioned honestly, "You want to live here? You got an old hardware store that charges twice of what Home Depot does, one restaurant with a rattle snake as a waitress, I mean how's anyone suppose to make a living here?"

When raised in such environmental conditions, finding ways to adaptively cope with the stressors can be equally challenging. "Social support networks (i.e.

extended family) ameliorate the hardships faced by many low-income rural families" (Mammen, et al., 2015, p. 447). Having the support of family can create an atmosphere of comfort and security. Feeling that one is able to rely upon others during difficult times for support can ease the exposure of chronic stressors. Toby found such support from his brother Tanner when he devised a plan to commit bank robberies to obtain funds to save his family's land from foreclosure. Toby learned that his brother's support was unconditional when he asked him, "Then why in the hell did you agree to do it?" Tanner responded, "Because you asked, little brother."

Others find that the support of family and friends is absent or insufficient in providing adequate assistance through these difficult hardships. For many, there is a desire to escape and try to obtain success; and at the very least, a different way of living elsewhere. Upon crossing ranchers running from wildfires, one noted,

> I ought it just turn me to ashes, put me out of my misery…. the 21$^{st}$ century and racing a fire and a river with a herd of cattle….and I wonder why my kids won't do this shit for a living.

The requirements, difficulties, and stress that accompany the employment of a rancher can be deterrents to new generations where they lack a desire to commit to such lifestyle. Despite gaining an inheritance, similarly, when Toby shared with his son, Justin, acted by John-Paul Howard, that he and his brother owned the ranch, his son asked, "What am I suppose to do with a ranch?" To his son's surprise, his father added, "We found oil on it. You and your brother ain't gonna have to worry about money anymore." This shift in the ability to access resources from what had been an infertile ground allowed for the family and next generations a chance to exit their existing state of poverty. Finding oil, in essence, liquid gold, for these families created an opportunity to reap financial security again; and for many, to obtain financial security for the first time.

"Poverty is a complex phenomenon" (Mammen, et al., 2015, p. 447). It is a condition that "implies the absence of wellbeing due to a set of deficiencies that threaten the physical and psychological integrity of those suffering from it" (Palomar Lever, et al., 2005, p. 376). This environmental experience creates stress upon individuals that impacts one cognitively, emotionally, and psychologically. "These psychological processes are generated by economic deprivation itself" (Sakamoto, et al, 2014, p. 206). Of hope, the psychological consequences of poverty do not have to continue across one's lifespan and the benefits can be transmitted through generations. In particular, once securing their family's estate and gaining oil from their land, the Howard family was left with hope that their financial future had promise. In turn, the psychological compromises of yesteryear that poverty fostered promised to diminish into the Howard family's history, where Toby declared, "not my boys, not anymore."

BEST PSYCHOLOGY IN FILM

## *MARCUS HAMILTON*

Performed by: Jeff Bridges

*RETIREMENT*

> *"I often think about dogs when I think about work and retirement. There are many breeds of dog that just need to be working, and useful, or have a job of some kind, in order to be happy. Otherwise they are neurotically barking, scratching, or tearing up the sofa. A working dog needs to work. And I am a working dog.*
>
> – Martha Sherrill

Marcus Hamilton, a police detective arriving to his "golden years," was presented with his final police work: to solve a case of bank robberies that occurred in West Texas. The Howard brother's mass crime spree engaged Marcus in what he did best, understanding criminal minds to solve crimes. As Marcus navigated the close of his professional career, he was conflicted by what he anticipated retirement would bring. Specifically, he believed that he would engage in "sitting on the porch practicing my future," as he shared with his partner Alberto. "Most retirees are concerned with the possibility that their retirement years would be useless and nonproductive" (Guzman, et al., 2008, p. 760). Marcus, similar to those in his same age cohort feared that once retired he would have little to occupy his time and thoughts. And though he realized that the time had come to end his career, Marcus was unwilling "to go quietly to their golf courses or beach homes in Florida" (Gibaldi, 2013 p. 51). Rather, he worked to create vivid memories for his coworkers to remember him prior to his retirement.

Marcus relied upon his social interactions to make this imprint. Creating memories of Marcus included engaging with him interpersonally, which caused one to be vulnerable to statements that were politically incorrect; making comment to one's ethnic and racial background. For Marcus, these interactions primarily held with his partner were made as a way to ensure that Alberto would hold him in mind once he retired. Marcus commented to Alberto, "in a year's time, it's my teasing that you gonna miss, it's the thing you're gonna laugh about when you stand over my grave."

Equally, Marcus relied upon the use of ethnic epithets defensively. When making such statements, Marcus used humor, though in poor taste, to "tease" Alberto. For example, rather than continue to pontificate with Alberto regarding the activities that he could engage in during retirement to entertain him, Marcus resorted to shifting the topic of discussion. Instead, he made a statement that would pull for frustration and other negative emotions from Alberto in an effort to deflect his fears of his new life. Alberto noted, "I don't know how you are gonna survive without someone to outsmart. You need a hobby and quick." Alberto continued by suggesting to Marcus various activities to participate in to occupy his retirement, such as, "You like to fish," where Marcus barked in response, "not enough to do it every goddamn day." It is common that "much of the American ritual of retirement stresses separation of this part of life from earlier adulthood" (Albert, 2002, p. 339). Marcus struggled to conceptualize what his life would be like during retirement other than wasting days away in a rocking chair.

Within recent years, the Baby Boomer generation that are currently within their retirement ages have experienced a new frontier once entering this stage. This generation has not been found to enter into retirement as their parents and other generations had. Instead, "about half of all American adults say they feel younger than their actual age" (Gibaldi, 2013 p. 50). "The threshold of what used to be considered the 'golden years'. This was traditionally a time when people started to retire" (Gibaldi, 2013 p. 51). In 2017, "nowadays it is more widely understood that old age does not necessarily mean decrepitude and disability" (Lillyman & Land, 2007, p. 28). Because of this understanding, "older people are expected to maintain roles they have occupied throughout their adult lives" (Albert, 2002, p. 338).

Additionally, because older individuals feel more youthful, they "are excited to retire and reach a period of life where they are able to focus on family and pursue other personal hobbies and interests" (Gibaldi, 2013 p. 51). Many interface with their retirement years by "seek[ing] definite breaks from their careers" (Albert, 2002, p. 339). Frequently, retirees engage in activities that were uncommonly participated in while working to mark their retirement. For instance, one can

> use a period of travel to mark separation of the work and nonwork portions of their lives, clean out vestiges of their prior lives by going through papers and possessions, separating what is valuable from what is not, and craft their post-work lives so as not to be victims of successful careers but failed retirements (Albert, 2002, p. 339).

Retirees may feel excited to embark on this phase of life and can also feel the pressures of confirming that they are using this time effectively. For retirees can feel that "all betray a commonly held but not quite articulated sense that, if not properly managed, retirement will kill you" (Albert, 2002, p. 339).

In reality, retirees face the unknown when entering this stage of life. Transitioning into new territory can create fears and uncertainties. Nguyen found that "fears about growing old significantly negatively predicted both life satisfaction and overall retirement satisfaction" (2014, p. 115). His research also yielded that retirees possessed "fears regarding loss of their independence or liberty, especially loss of mobility" (2014, p. 115). Lillyman & Land gained similar findings; and in addition found that "people also noted a fear of losing mental capacity, losing a driving license, paying for care, loss of a partner, etc." (Lillyman & Land, 2007, p. 27). "Hence this period of freedom and opportunity is also fraught with anxiety and concern" (Albert, 2002, p. 339).

In order to mitigate concerns regarding retiring, individuals may engulf themselves into specific activities to remain active. "One dimension is the value assigned to maintaining social relationships and productive activities even as a person's physical and cognitive abilities decline" (Albert, 2002, p. 338). Guzman and colleagues reported, "retirement can provide vast opportunities for family activities and involvement. Such opportunities may even be an incentive for retiring" (2008, p. 759). Additionally, engaging with "friends, likewise, are especially meaningful in old age" (Guzman, et al., 2008, p. 760). Other activities may also occupy those who are retired. For example, "religiosity tends to drive away fears and anxieties that an individual experiences because religion increases self-esteem, reduces depression, and enhances life satisfaction," and "for many older people, religion gives meaning to life" (Guzman, et al., 2008, p. 758).

Despite being capable of including oneself into social interests, many retirees encounter challenges with being able to fully engage in retirement. Past career pursuits continue to haunt days, and desires to "find peace" is sought. Marcus continued to struggle with the idea of retirement, even once ending his employment. According to Alberto, Marcus attempted to prolong his final case to avoid entering this phase in life. "You trying to make this last as long as you can, because the longer it lasts, the farther you are from that front porch," said

Alberto. Marcus later suggested that rather than retire, "who knows, maybe one of these bank robbers is gonna want a gunfight and I can dodge my retirement in a blaze of glory." At the conclusion of the film, Marcus' final act as a police officer became an accomplishment noted on the news. Even still, Marcus' personality and strength of understanding the criminal mind left him with questions regarding specifics of the crime. As a result, though retired and spent time rocking in a chair on his front porch, thoughts regarding the case visited him. In response, Marcus initiated a visit to the police precinct to gain answers.

"Hey, Marcus, aren't you suppose to be retired?" officers asked when he walked through the police stations doors.

"How's life as a civilian?" his former colleague asked.

"Well, you know," Marcus was able to muster.

Once he asked to take a "peek" at Tanner Howard's file, he acknowledged,

"I ain't got nothing better to do."

His prior colleague takes time to inform him of the status of the case and remind him that he is retired. Thereafter, Marcus' curiosity drove him to the home of Toby Howard, where he directly confronted him regarding the crimes. Marcus was able to admit that he understood why his brother would commit such crimes, but could not understand his motives to participate. With an invitation from Toby to continue the conversation in the future, Marcus accepted his offer, "I'd like that. I'll be seeing you." Marcus' interest in visiting Toby at a different date provided a sense of security that his work of investigation indeed had not come to an end.

**What Makes This Character Rich?**

Immediately within the film, Marcus' age and wisdom are both highlighted. It is noted that Marcus is on the precipice of retiring and he thrives on attempting to understand the inner workings of crimes by understanding the criminal. The internal conflict that he experienced regarding closing his career and saying goodbye to a position that he gleaned great satisfaction was a constant struggle throughout scenes.

During his last assignment, Marcus desired to illustrate to his partner, Alberto, that his skills and talents remained relevant. Consequently, Marcus placed a great deal of his efforts into solving his last case. He invested significant time and energy investigating the robbers. He insisted that he and Alberto remain in hotels in various towns to ensure that they would be close to where the next robbery may occur. Marcus sat on porches until dawn as a lookout. Marcus' commitment to his work was exceptional and unwavering. As such, even after his retirement, he remained thoughtful regarding aspects of the case that he could not readily prove.

Emotionally, Marcus attempted to evade negative feelings that arose regarding anticipating retirement. In particular, he entertained himself with the defense of humor, a higher order defense (Gabbard, 2005), which provided him an outlet to experience positive feelings during his final days as sheriff. Of interest, Marcus' use of humor tended to devalue Alberto's ethnicity by uttering epithets that caused Alberto to become annoyed with him. In response to Marcus, Alberto reminded him that his time as sheriff was limited, that "in three weeks you can watch whatever you want on TV" and noted that he did not intend to miss him after he departed. Marcus' interpretations of his interactions with Alberto were of endearment. Though Alberto anticipated Marcus' deprecating statements would be recalled in the future as such, in the moment, it created an atmosphere that caused Alberto to desire for Marcus to discontinue his behaviors. Despite stating blatant upsetting comments to Alberto, Marcus' affection toward him was elucidated based upon the concern he had for his physical wellbeing illustrated by his final act as sheriff.

Fear of the unknown remained within the foreground in each scene we find Marcus. In some ways, the privilege Marcus possessed in being able to retire and the anxiety that accompanied this stage in his life paralleled the anxiety the Howard boys experienced as a result of poverty within their lives; all parties questioned the trajectory of their future. Marcus' anxiety displayed great vulnerability in his character, which furnished an opportunity for audiences to favor him despite his numerous offenses issued towards his partner. The duality of Marcus' character that creates both empathy and frustration within audiences offers a delicate illustration of the complexity of humans.

BEST PSYCHOLOGY IN FILM

## *HIDDEN FIGURES*

Directed by: Theodore Melfi

## *SCENE I*

*A young girl walks down a rubble street, kicking rocks.*

**KATHERINE:** "14, 15, 16, prime, 18, prime, 20, 21, 22, prime..."

*Mr. Smithson sits at a desk. Ms. Sumner walks and stands next to him. Katherine's parents Joylette and Joshua Coleman sit in two wooden chairs in front of the desk.*

**MR. SMITHSON:** "West Virginia Collegiate Institute is the best school for Negros in the state."

**MS. SUMNER:** "It's the only school passed the eighth grade anywhere near here."

*Noting upon her observations of a stain glass window while waiting for her parents.*

**KATHERINE:** "Isosceles. Scalene. Equilateral. Rhombus. Trapezoid…"

**MR. COLEMAN:** "Katherine's in the sixth grade."

**MS. SUMNER:** "They want to take her early."

**KATHERINE:** "Tetrahedron. Dodecahedron…"

**MS. SUMNER:** "They're offering a full scholarship. All you have to do is get there."

*Katherine's parents look at one another surprised.*

*ACKNOWLEDGMENT*

> *"It is not our differences that divide us. It is our inability to recognize, accept, and celebrate those differences."*
> –Audre Lorde, *Our Dead Behind Us: Poems*

All was a buzz at the arrival of the film *Hidden Figures*. Once viewing, interest in women calculators of the West Calculators of National Aeronautics and Space Administration (NASA), who contributed to performing mathematical computations that enabled the first astronaut to orbit the earth and land on the moon, grew astronomically. Consensus of the public noted that these women and their accomplishments had gone vastly unrecognized and "hidden" for more than fifty years in the United States. Though on Tuesday November 24, 2015, Katherine Johnson, a NASA calculator, who was instrumental in the above mentioned world events for her mathematical abilities and contributions, was honored by President Obama and awarded the Presidential Medal of Freedom. Approximately one year thereafter on December 25, 2016, the film *Hidden Figures* was released in cinemas in the United States. This film shared with the public the story of three women within the West Calculator's department. Found within the scenes of this cinematic work, based upon true events, *Hidden Figures* delivered a novel, informative and inspiring account to audiences.

It is noted that within most chapters of this book, psychological dynamics of discussed films are explored in isolation to additional dynamics that can be discovered belonging to other fields and areas of study. However, *Hidden Figures* highlighted social and interpersonal dynamics that influenced the observation of the psychological factors greatly. Thus, understanding the psychology within this film is dependent upon a closer examination of such non-psychological factors that intersect with psychology. For instance, *Hidden Figures* depicted events that were based in 1961 when the United States' social climate was engaged in various transitional movements. To name a few, the Civil Rights movement was active in social and political change for the country. The NASA space program was within its infancy competing with other space programs around the world (i.e. Russia) to be the first to perform actions that were once thought to be impossible. Additionally, the American Feminist movement was in its early stages. As America was in transition regarding human rights issues, women, and women of color in particular, faced adversities that significantly impacted their ability to obtain work.

At this time in history, in the United States, challenges for women of color were commonplace. Women of color were provided limited resources to perform work duties. Within the workplace they were expected to adhere to Jim Crow laws and subject themselves to less that humane conditions provided to men: specifically, Caucasian men. Consequently, within the segregated state of Virginia in which the film illustrated work life at Langley, the West Calculators faced challenges to be treated in the same fashion as their counterparts. For examples, various opportunities were not extended due to their race and gender. Attempts to obtain further education that would support advancement required court approval to modify the legal standards. Work duties were unrecognized, which resulted in lack of job title appropriations and financial increases that reflected competency and work performed. Capable individuals lacked recognition for talents and contributions; and when provided, appraisals were limited. Further, many times, protocols for women performing specific actions at NASA had yet to be created; thus these professional women were required to forge change. Their presence shifted the status quo and forced social movement within their work environments. In the event the West Calculators became complacent, both technological and psychological growth would have suffered significantly. For the women described within the film, Katherine G. Johnson, performed by Tarji P. Henson, Dorothy Vaughan (Octavia Spencer), and Mary Jackson acted by Janelle Monae, faced similar obstacles that directly impacted their ability to accomplish work tasks efficiently. As these women navigated a Caucasian-male-dominated environment, they fought to receive courtesies, respect, and the recognition that was earned based upon their performance.

"By working, individuals contribute not only to the material reproduction of their society, but also to the formation of their own identity" (Angella, 2016, p. 342). Working in an environment where support from superiors is scarce and promotions for work well done are lacking, how might this work environment impact both job performance and overall wellbeing? "An increasing number of studies emphasize the crucial role of non-monetary incentives as driver of labor productivity" (Grolleau, Mzoughi & Pekovic, 2015, p. 508). Such non-monetary incentives include providing praise and positive acknowledgements for specific job-related behaviors. Additionally, "numerous studies and articles in the management press frequently emphasizes that a top motivator of employee performance is recognition" (Grolleau, et al., 2015, p. 509). "As a result, at present both common sense and empirical evidence leads managers to conclude that recognition programs are highly effective motivational instruments" (Feys, Ansell & Wille, 2012, p. 492).

Within *Hidden Figures*, challenges with providing recognition in the workplace were evident in each of the main character's narrative. Katherine Johnson, known for her superior ability to perform sophisticated mathematical calculations amongst her peers, was tried numerous times and in a myriad of ways by her colleagues when transferred to the Space Test Group of the Space Task Force. Initially, due to racial prejudices, upon her arrival, her colleagues supplied her with a coffee pot labeled "Colored" to acknowledge which pot was appropriate for her use based upon her race. Despite contributing significantly to the progress of the Space Test Group's missions, she was instructed that her role as a calculator did not allow her to take ownership of her products. Rather, she was repeatedly instructed to remove her name from briefing reports she submitted to her superiors regarding her formulations. Further, due to her gender, Ms. Johnson was forbade from attending meetings that both discussed her completed work and provided necessary information that guided the trajectory of her future assignments. She produced consistent superior work, proved to be a competent peer, and was relied upon by the department to produce figures that were crucial in early space launches. Still, she continued to have difficulty generating positive relationships with her colleagues and was treated with consistent disrespect due to her gender and race.

Dorothy Vaughan, the acting supervisor of the West Calculators, also experienced similar challenges. For some time, Ms. Vaughan was charged to perform the work of a supervisor, although she was denied the proper promotion that would recognize her duties. Because of a lack of title to accurately reflect her work, she also was denied the financial compensation warranted for her labor. In an effort to ensure her and her colleagues remained relevant to NASA once the first International Business Machines (IBM's) were introduced, Ms. Vaughan became self-taught to master computer programming. Only once she learned this essential skill that assisted the Space Task Force was she awarded the promotion to supervisor and her performance was acknowledged.

Lastly, Mary Jackson was shown as a young, aspiring engineer. In order to actualize this dream, she was required to further her education. As a woman of color, she would be the first to attend such classes towards earning this specific degree in Virginia. In order to gain approval to further her education, Ms. Jackson had to petition the Virginia court and convince the judge that her being the first woman of color to pursue this education would result in a significant impact on world events. Successfully doing so, she was permitted the attendance with the limitation of enrolling in night classes only. Her matriculation resulted in her becoming the first woman-of-color engineer employed at NASA.

Research suggests that providing praise within the workplace has direct benefits to promote job performance. It is naturally believed that "superstars," individuals who have attained extraordinary achievements, "can serve as role models to others, inspiring and motivating them to do their utmost best" (Lockwood & Kunda, 1997, p. 91). Individuals who are likely to view themselves similar to others tend to believe that they are equally able to receive similar recognition, status, and rewards as the "superstar" (Lockwood and Kunda, 1997).

> Hence, we expect that when one of two colleagues in a high quality relationship (where similarities exist between two co-workers) receives positive recognition, the other will feel good because the person believes (s)he might be able to gain the same recognition (Feys & Anseel, 2012, p. 494).

Additionally, individuals who share attributes who have close, high quality relationships can feel positively when their peers are provided accolades for their performance by a "pride of association with the other" (Lockwood & Kunda,

1997, p. 93). In preference to feeling deflated, the person feels honored to belong to a group of colleagues who produce superior work.

Providing recognition also makes for new challenges to rise to the surface. Specifically, recognition within the workplace for those who work in groups or teams can invite the presence of a lack of group cohesion, feelings of envy and competitive dynamics. Feys and Anseel (2012) reported that Long and Shields (2010) "were among the first to challenge the dominant assumption in the literature, claiming that non-cash recognition programs are not problem free." Alternatively, when employees are provided non-monetary acknowledgement, the work environment dynamic shifts and accolades, praise, and acknowledgement "may cause an atmosphere of 'winners' and 'losers'" (p. 493). Our culture also "holds the cliché, that superstars can demoralize and deflate less outstanding others" (Lockwood & Kunda, 1997, p. 91).

Further, when one feels that the outstanding individual who receives praise appears "relevant," (where one is able to compare themselves with the individual; yet finds a discrepancy between the person's belief that accomplishments of the other are attainable to the same level of success), one may experience discouragement. The accomplished individual's success "highlights one's own failures and shortcomings" (Lockwood and Kunda, 1997, p. 93). When the individual who is perceived as "different" begins to receive praise from superiors, rather than experience positive feelings for the individual, the recognition ensues feelings of concern due to the lack of similar attributes that earned the praise. Consequently, this discomfort can begin to disrupt the original workplace dynamics.

Feys and Anseel (2012) found that "other's positive recognition led to the highest amounts of negative emotions when the quality of the relationship was low" (p. 503). When one does not have a positive relationship with the individual receiving praise, negative emotions can surface. Baumeister, Smart & Boden (1996) posited that aggressive, problematic, and violent behavior can be demonstrated within such environments. When one who is equally or more talented has entered the work environment, one may feel a sense that there is a threat to one's own capabilities. In turn, the individual is perceived as a threat to one's self-esteem. For those who possess a high self-esteem, "most of the time they scarcely think about the possibility that they will lose esteem, and so it is only when a threat emerges that they become defensive" (Baumeister, 1996, p. 8). Of further concern, these authors suggest that "when favorable views about oneself are questioned, contradicted, impugned, mocked, challenged, or otherwise put in jeopardy, people may aggress…they will aggress against the source of threat" (Baumeister, et al., p. 8) in an effort to regulate their feelings of fear. However, these unregulated emotions lend themselves to create interpersonal dynamics where "gaining esteem requires taking it away from others" (Baumeister, 1996, p. 11). In lieu of engaging in self-introspection to examine one's strengths and weaknesses, one's hostilities may become a fertile ground for acting out; and taking one's negative feelings out on the source of a perceived threat (the accomplished other).

The collegial relationship Katherine Johnson and Paul Stafford (performed by Jim Parsons) shared was riddled with discord. Upon first glance of Katherine, Paul wondered regarding her role to the Space Task Force. When unable to conceive that she would perform calculations and check his and other's work for accuracy, he attempted to make her work more challenging by redacting information that she required to perform her work effectively. The differences in attributes between Katherine and Paul were acute. Between the two, gender, race, and ethnicity were amongst the characteristics overtly observable. These dissimilar attributes were of significance to Paul, which hindered him from being able to interact with Katherine as an equal. Paul preferred to ignore her presence. When unable to do so, his interactions involved providing her a lack of eye contact and conversing with her in a dismissive manner. He used short sentences and spoke with a firm authoritarian voice. For Paul, the difference between himself and Katherine was so great that he lacked motivation to invest in generating a genuine relationship with her as a colleague.

According to reviews, *Hidden Figures* is a film described as a "feel-good biographical drama" (Chen, 2016) that is "empowerment cinema at its most populist, and one only wishes that the film had existed at the time it depicts" (Debruge, 2016). Even in present day, particular scenes evoke discomfort to view, provoke tears to fall and sadness to build due to the discrimination the women experienced, unfair treatment they received and pain they endured. As with all of the women's narratives within the film, Katherine Johnson, Dorothy Vaughn, and Mary Jackson's excellence was demonstrated by their commitment and intellectual brilliance. Their contributions to the Space Task Force were undeniable, enabling America's space travel to be the first to achieve the impossible tasks of its time. As trials were presented, these women displayed extraordinary patience and navigated turbulences with grace. Despite feelings of disappointment and waivered hope, the West Calculators continuously exhibited determination and perseverance within the social movements of the year of 1961.

*DOROTHY VAUGHN*

Performed by: Octavia Spencer

BEST PSYCHOLOGY IN FILM

***DEFENDED***

> *"I'm tough, I'm ambitious, and I know exactly what I want. If that makes me a bitch, okay."*
>
> –Madonna

The power of psychological defense mechanisms can be the determinate of one's failure or one's success. Defense mechanisms, "a defensive reaction by an organism" and for the purpose of this literature, "an often unconscious mental process (such as repression) that makes possible compromise solutions to personal problems" (Merriam-Webster Dictionary, 2017) are responses that can behoove or jeopardize one's future positive results. Defenses are initiated typically to avoid conscious conflict or anxiety and are protective devices to increase the chance of survival. Due to various obstacles that Ms. Dorothy Vaughn, acted by Octavia Spencer, faced within the film of *Hidden Figures*, she utilized numerous defense mechanisms to assist her in a challenging work environment that enabled her to experience success.

Defense mechanisms, are protecting factors that everyone possesses (Gabbard, 2055). "Virtually any psychological process can be used defensively, and so no summary of the defenses can be complete" (McWilliams, 2011, p. 126; Brenner, 1982). The type of defenses that are available for use vary and are used to protect "against the unpleasure of anxiety and depressive affect, against their ideational content, or against both" (Brenner, 1982, p. 9).

According to psychodynamic models, defense mechanisms vary in effectiveness to reduce unpleasant affect. Depending upon how the mechanisms are utilized determines whether the use of the specific defenses will be helpful or harmful. Defenses "are classified according to a hierarchy from the most immature or pathological to the most mature and healthy" (Gabbard, 2005, p 34). Primitive, immature defenses "operate in a global, undifferentiated way" (McWilliams, 2011, p. 102) and influence one's total sensory experience, affect, thoughts, and behaviors. Mature and higher-order defenses include "more sophisticated means of processing anxiety and assimilating a complex and disturbing reality" (McWilliams, 2011, p. 103). When defenses are insufficient in warding off unpleasant emotions, one will continue to experience discomfort in the form of anxiety, sadness, frustration, hurt, shame, etc. However, when one is able to activate the use of a defensive mechanism that is suitable for the situation, one is relieved from the feelings of discomfort. Consequently, the individual is freed of the associated negative affect and able to continue to function ordinary without burden. Generally, psychologically healthier individuals rely upon the use of numerous mature defenses to manage stressful times, varying the use of the defense mechanisms in their repertoire (McWilliams, 2011).

Dorothy Vaughn was introduced as a capable mechanic. At the onset of the film she was found under her vehicle assessing the source of its immobility. Once interrupted by police, she determined that she must override the starter for the vehicle to become functional. However, the officer asked for identification and noted that he was unaware of the presence of specific individuals who worked at NASA. Prior to the officer identifying the type of individual he had in mind, Dorothy interrupted and informed that many women were employed with the space programs at NASA. In her doing so, she assisted the officer to displace any anticipated negative emotions he had regarding race onto women globally. Her ability to guide the officer required her to personally utilize the defense mechanism of suppression, where she was able to "consciously decide not to attend to a particular feeling, state or impulse" (Gabbard, 2015, p. 37). In anticipating the officer's ignorance of women of color working at NASA, hearing him address their race may have evoked feelings of discomfort in her. To reduce such negative affect, Dorothy was successfully able to curtail the chance of being offended by gingerly redirecting the source of her anticipated discomfort.

Shortly thereafter, Dorothy was observed at her place of employment managing the assignments of a team of women computers. Working as a supervisor in the absence of the formal title, she approached her superior to inquire regarding her application to formalize her current role. When she was alerted that she would not be granted the position, Dorothy advocated for the need of a supervisor for the team coupled with her concern that her efforts were not accurately recognized for the work she performed. Dorothy's acknowledgement of the unfair situation to her supervisor ensured that they both understood that she lacked recognition of her work in the current arrangement. Unsurprisingly, this work relationship evoked feelings of frustration for Dorothy. In reaction, she found support in venting in an uncensored manner to her two trusted coworkers. She conveyed her feelings of frustration using a firm heightened toned voice with rapid speech. Though her friends supported her and agreed that her situation was unfair, it provided limited comfort. To assuage these negative feelings, Dorothy relied upon two defense mechanisms, identification and rationalization to lessen the intensity of her emotions.

Identification, the ability to "link with an object to restore self-esteem and self-cohesion to reduce anxiety, grief and shame" allowed Dorothy to connect with her friends and the women of her group who also produced work of excellence. Additionally, the use of rationalization, the understanding that negative events are not "so bad" in retrospect (McWilliams, 2011) is generally accessible to individuals whom are creative and intelligent as they are able to perceive situations in varying ways to make the best of situations in the absence of resentment (Gabbard, 2005). As Dorothy voiced her frustrations, she admitted, "And watching you two move on. Now don't get me wrong, any upward movement is movement for us all; just isn't movement for me." Noting that she witnessed her friends who possessed similar talents move forward allowed her to remain connected to those whom she identified with professionally. Dorothy also utilized rationalizing, stating that their success assisted all, including herself globally as a woman and of color. Such recognition of her friend's status enabled her to view that her specific circumstance was "not so bad."

Sophisticated thought processes support the use of mature defense mechanisms such as anticipation and sublimation. As technology increased, the advantage of human computers was less essential. To remain relevant, Dorothy anticipated the needs of the space program and began self-educating herself in the skills necessary to remain an asset. Though her current work demands did not include learning how to program the first computer hardware of NASA, Dorothy invested her personal time to gain resources from the local library, faced continued discrimination and "delay[ed] immediate gratification by planning and thinking of future achievements and accomplishments" (Gabbard, 2005, p. 37). Additionally, her anticipation of employment attrition once the computer systems were established allowed her to transform her anxiety into productive action by the use of sublimation, "a creative, healthful, socially acceptable or beneficial resolution of internal conflicts between primitive urges and inhibiting forces" (McWilliams, 2011, p. 147).

Further, Dorothy Vaughn presented as a compassionate person, one willing to commit to further development as well as to the welfare of others. Within the film, though her friend Katherine Johnson was required to work late hours, Dorothy waited for her in the lot to provide transportation to her home. She also remained a dedicated advocate for the needs of the women she supervised. Dorothy's commitment "to the needs of others over and above one's own needs" (Gabbard, 2005, p. 37) was illustrated when she was eventually promoted to supervisor of the IBM computers group. At that time, she was willing to decline the forlorn promotion if she was unable to transfer her co-workers into IBM computer positions where she would likely be capable of securing their professional future at NASA.

Due to her use of primarily mature defense mechanisms, Dorothy Vaughn was able to articulate her frustrations, manage her anxieties, and continue to succeed and support others in their success. As literature supports, exhibiting psychological health depends upon the use of a number of mature ways to cope with anxiety while integrating challenging times into one's life. In the face of various prejudices related to race and gender, Dorothy's ability to attune to her frustrations and successfully use defensive mechanisms fostered opportunities for many fellow women of color while supporting numerous gains in science and technology.

**What Makes This Character Rich?**

Dorothy's presentation of a sincere, honest, yet pleasantly confrontational individual crafted the complexities within this role. When presented with challenges, she evaded conflict and clarified that she did not wish for trouble.

Though when difficult situations were unavoidable, Dorothy took initiative to create resolutions that would be in the best service to herself and others.

Further, Dorothy relied upon a host of higher-order and mature defense mechanisms that assisted her in navigating many unpleasant, "unfair" situations. Whether being rejected for a promotion or being told she could not access a book in a particular section of the library due to her race, Dorothy managed these painful disappointments in a psychologically mature fashion. Her ability to access a sophisticated range of defense mechanisms in her repertoire facilitated her ability to cope with difficulties with ease, freeing her from becoming disabled by fear and anxiety. These defenses fostered success in integrating her emotions, granting her the capacity to expend emotional energies on the advancements of herself and others.

Interpersonally, Dorothy confronted those who fostered adversities and unfairness that continued to promote prejudices. Acknowledging her strong beliefs, she advocated for her beliefs in a manner that resulted in interactions with others that remained pleasant while leaving both parties privy to understand that injustices existed. For example, Dorothy's boss, Mrs. Mitchell (performed by Kirsten Dunst) stated:

**MS. MITCHELL:** "Despite what you may think, I have nothing against yawl."

**DOROTHY:** "I know. I know you probably believe that."

Her ability to rely upon truths coupled with pleasantries, while managing her negative affect effectively enabled her to engage in sincere interactions with others.

Dorothy Vaughn proved to be a talented mathematician, an advocate, and servicewoman who promoted others. Her ability to genuinely describe acts of discrimination in a thought-provoking manner while managing her personal strong emotions displayed a model to successfully manage negative affect and internal conflicts.

BEST PSYCHOLOGY IN FILM

## *LA LA LAND*

Directed by Damien Chazelle

## *SCENE I*

*Cars parked on the interstate. Songs come from each car. Stuck in traffic, a woman in a car begins to sing and leaves her car. Others follow to sing and dance to "Another Day of Sun". The song concludes.*

"WINTER"

*Camera focuses upon Sebastian in his car. He is in traffic listening to jazz music. He frequently rewinds a tape cassette in the dash of his car. Camera pans and lands on Mia in her car with her phone to her ear.*

**MIA:** "No, I swear to God. She was wrecked. She was completely wrecked! I know. I know. It was pure insanity. It's insanity? Ah!"

*Mia slams her phone on the passenger seat and refers to a script.*

**MIA:** "Lunacy. It was pure lunacy."

*A loud horn blares. Mia looks into her rearview mirror and sees Sebastian shaking his head with his lips pursed. Sebastian drives around Mia's car, stops and stares at her. Mia raises her middle finger at him. Sebastian drives away.*

**MIA:** "What's his problem? I should go."

# *EMERGING ADULTHOOD*

> *"Don't you find it odd,"* she continued,
> *"that when you're a kid, everyone, all the world,*
> *encourages you to follow your dreams. But when you're*
> *older, somehow they act offended if you even try."*
> -Ethan Hawke, The Hottest State

Maturing is a challenging part of life. At each developmental stage, new tasks are required to become better equipped to approach the world. In America, developmental stages have historically included infancy, toddler, childhood, early school age, middle school age, adolescence, and adulthood as typical milestones that are enjoyed and endured. Each stage brings about unique challenges to master, where skills are acquired that help shape a person and their ability to navigate their environment. As the world changes, so does the demands placed upon individuals as they mature. Emerging adulthood (EA), a period that describes the years concluding the teenage years to the period of the mid-twenties, is a developmental stage in which $21^{st}$ century psychologists are adopting to describe the stage in life when individuals' exit adolescence and transition into adulthood responsibilities. Sebastian, performed by Ryan Gosling, and Mia (acted by Emma Stone) together within the film *La La Land* portrayed young adults on the cusp of exiting the EA developmental stage whilst facing difficulties to fully launch into the following stage of young adulthood.

In 2004, Jeffery Jensen Arnett proposed the theory supporting the presence of EA. Within his authored book entitled, *Emerging Adulthood: The Winding Road from the Late Teens through the Twenties,* the theory outlined that EA developmental stage encompasses individuals "from the late teens through the mid to late 20s (roughly 12-25)" (Arnett, 2007, p. 68). He posited that the trajectory of one's development had evolved since the mid 20$^{th}$ century; suggesting that previous life stages best articulated the life of individuals engaged "in industrialized societies" whom were married and "entered stable full-time work by around age 20 or shortly after" (Arnett, 2007, p. 68). This paradigm of development was considered antiquated and no longer matched current normative behavioral patterns of individuals within this age range. For example, at present "median ages of marriage had risen into the late 20s, and the early to mid-20s became a time of frequent job changes and, for many people, pursuit of postsecondary education or training" (Arnett, 2007, p. 68-69).

Since the introduction of the EA developmental stage, this theory has piqued the interest of a range of disciplines "including psychology, psychiatry, sociology, anthropology, education, epidemiology, health sciences, human development, geography, nursing, social work, philosophy, pediatrics, family studies, journalism and law" (Arnett, 2007, p. 68). EA is "the age of identity explorations, the age of instability, the self-focused age, the age of feeling in-between, and the age of possibilities" according to Arnett (2007, p. 69). Cinematically, this developmental stage has captivated audiences and has brought dramatic tales of these years to the screen. Popular films have highlighted the EA developmental stage and the process in which decisions regarding career, love, and life occur within this stage. Films such as *How to be Single* (2016), directed by Christian Ditter, *Brown Sugar* (2002), directed by Rick Famuyiwa, and *We are Your Friends* (2015), directed by Max Joseph, illustrate the universality of this development stage that occurs across gender and ethnicity. These films capture negotiations of love, decisions regarding career(s), and learning oneself. In 2016, this developmental stage was featured in *La La*

*Land*, a film incorporating characteristics of EA accompanied by song and dance that dazzled viewers.

At the conclusion of adolescence there is a range of time that is characterized by "identity exploration and possessing feelings of instability" (Peer & McAuslan, 2015, p. 176). During the EA stage, individuals begin to have the opportunity to obtain life dreams and commit to aspirations that feel attainable to pursue into adulthood. "Emerging adults enjoy their self-focused freedom from role obligations and restraints, and they take satisfaction in their progress toward self-sufficiency" (Arnett, 2007, p. 70). Working in a coffee shop as a barista on the Warner Brothers lot, Mia sees a famous actress order coffee and is inspired that one day she would be able to fulfill her dream of becoming an actress. As she rehearsed and auditioned, Mia worked to solidify her career and attempted to better understand herself. At the onset of the film, Mia isolated herself from her friends, looked in the mirror and sang, "somewhere there's a place, where I find who I'm going to be," a lyric emphasizing the stage of personal exploration and creating a future for oneself.

Similarly, Sebastian conceptualized himself as a committed musician; one who desired to remain loyal to performing classic jazz. Yet, he found himself constantly struggling to become financially stable when his passions did not equate to steady employment. Sebastian strived to find work that "not only pays well but also provides a satisfying and enjoyable identity fit" (Arnett, 2007, p. 71). Arnett further reported that these employment positions "are difficult for reality to match and often require compromises of their hopes and dreams" (2007). Sebastian encountered numerous moments that demonstrated for him that in order to obtain financial security, he would be required to make sacrifices and compromises from his original desires.

Due to the turbulent nature of emerging adulthood, when numerous questions are had regarding the direction of one's future, individuals can begin to experience various emotional responses. EA is also a stage of "optimism [that] frequently co-exists with an undercurrent of trepidation" (Arnett, 2007, p. 25). Individuals tend to have "the subjective experience of going through emerging adulthood (EA), which can include daunting perceptions of indecision and instability" which "may foster self-doubt" (Reifman & Grahe, 2016, p. 138). Specifically, self-doubt "refers to how certain a person feels about important abilities" (Hermann, et al., 2008, p. 396). "In other words, emerging adults may experience apprehension, skepticism, and doubt if they struggle with stability, autonomy, and feeling 'stuck in the middle' during this time of life" (Peer & McAuslan, 2015, p. 182).

"Self-doubt, however, reflects one's feeling of uncertainty about competence that may reach beyond a specific sense of performance efficacy" (Zhao & Wichman, 2015, p. 1). "Experiencing self-doubt could lead emerging adults to question their ability to successfully negotiate the normative features of development" (Peer & McAuslan, 2015, p. 176). As a result, "it is true that identity issues are prominent in emerging adulthood and that sorting through them and finding satisfying alternatives in love and work can generate anxiety" (Arnett, 2007, p. 70). "That is, the doubt about one's competence and self-worth could manifest itself in many forms, ranging from concern about one's ability level to feeling that one's worth is determined largely by performance" (Oleson, et al., 2000, p. 500). Mia was depicted as an EA tussling with hopes and dreams of how she would like to see her future as an adult. Upon auditions, Mia invested herself to present her best. The vulnerability she experienced upon each casting audition produced uncertainty in her talents and herself. Lacking callbacks, her confidence in her craft and the hope she possessed to become an actress waned.

Generally, "today's emerging adults are more confident and assertive than in the past, and that they have high expectations for their lives" (Arnett, 2007, p. 25). Despite their high regard and convictions, many times EA's appreciate external validation to support their development. Finally receiving a call back, she reported, "It's really exciting," which aided in rebuilding her belief in herself. EA is also a time where possibilities remain options, yet decisions are made to hone the direction one will travel.

> Perhaps the sheer number of possibilities available for emerging adults-trigger a sense of apprehension and/or skepticism about one's identity and one's future. This may lead to self-doubt among some emerging adults, and in turn disrupt their ability to effectively navigate the developmental dimensions associated with this time of life (Peer & McAuslan, 2015, p. 176).

Consequently, self-doubt where "attention to one's self, a focus on 'hesitation' and 'uncertainty,' and measuring oneself rather than fully engaging in tasks in an unselfconscious way" (Braslow, et.al., 2012, p. 472) plagues this stage of life. "Individuals high in self-doubt may spend a good deal of time thinking about their level of confidence, recalling both past and present illustrations" (Hermann, et al., 2002, p. 406). Further, EA individuals "may experience self-doubt, and when facing upcoming tasks, be fearful that they will fail" (Oleson, et al., 2000, p. 493). "People may experience doubts about their ability and their capacity to perform well as they approach and engage" in tasks and activities (Braslow, et.al., 2012, p. 475). Yet, within *La La Land*, Sebastian remained committed to his unique passions and continued to work towards his goals. Additionally, Mia honed in on her talents and passions and performed despite her anxieties and fears.

"There is little doubt that it takes longer to reach full adulthood today than it did in the past" (Arnett, 2007, p. 27). During this stage, emerging adults can "lack (or feel they lack) the confidence and wherewithal to succeed" (Reifman, et al., 2007, p. 4). Because the EA stage encompasses a host of life transitions, emerging adults tend to require external support to assist when they lack skills to be successful and experience difficult times. When Mia became disheartened by her failures in her career, she returned to her hometown and to her parent's residence to reevaluate her life's direction. Additionally, emerging adults frequently require prolonged assistance from parents and caring adults to help support their development. In fact, "large numbers of people (sometimes referred to as 'boomerang kids') are moving back in with their parents while exploring career directions" (Reifman, et al., 2007, p. 2). "Emerging adults are typically confused and glum, and overwhelmed by what the world seems to require from them" (Arnett, 2007, p. 24). Making firm decisions and following through until completion can be challenging when one is overcome with choices and demands felt to be overwhelming. This tends to be reflected in the attainment of higher education within university that "is often pursued in a nonlinear way, frequently combined with work, and punctuated by periods of nonattendance" (Arnett, 2000, p. 471).

"For most people, the late teens through the mid-twenties are the most volitional years of life" (Arnett, 2000, p. 469). These years include wrestling with who one is, who one will be and how one will succeed in becoming the ideal self. It is also "the most heterogeneous period of the life course because it is the least structured" (Arnett, 2007, p. 69). Every person has their own path to walk, personal struggles to be had and discoveries to be made. "By and large, emerging adults respond to the challenges of identity development not by collapsing into a quivering mass of fear but by making their way gradually toward laying the foundations for the adult life in love and work..." (Arnett, 2007, p. 24). Thus, and gratefully, "most people adapt successfully to its developmental challenges" (Arnett, 2007, p. 71) and progress through this stage into young adulthood with countless lessons learned.

BEST PSYCHOLOGY IN FILM

## *SEBASTIAN*

Performed by: Ryan Gosling

# *LOYALTY*

> *"We have to recognize that there cannot be relationships unless there is commitment, unless there is loyalty, unless there is love, patience, persistence."*
> Cornel West, *Breaking Bread: Insurgent Black Intellectual Life*

Many times when one perceives an individual as being loyal, the person is conceptualized to possess distinctive attributes. Being faithful to relationships and causes and remaining devoted despite circumstances commonly classifies loyal qualities. According to Merriam-Webster Dictionary, loyal is when one is capable of "giving or showing firm and constant support or allegiance to a person or institution." It is believed that loyal individuals will unconditionally provide support and their presence will be unwavering. As a result, being a staunch supporter of self or others is typically understood as a positive personality characteristic. However, when one is loyal, one may struggle to consider new information, adjust one's thoughts and beliefs, and make changes to one's behaviors due to the commitment to a specific individual or cause. In response, the loyal one may present as rigid and unable to be flexible in thought, hindering one's ability to adjust appropriately when needed. Sebastian, performed by Ryan Gosling, within the film *La La Land*, demonstrated the positive and negative impact loyalty can have and how these attributes may manifest in one's life based upon the ability to approach life circumstances with pliability.

Sebastian was introduced as a musician committed to his craft. He identified himself as a "serious musician," defined as an individual who appreciated and supported the traditional form of jazz. Despite being keenly aware that in current society there exist a small population who appreciate the traditional work, Sebastian's excitement to traditional jazz music was steadfast. He described to his girlfriend Mia, acted by Emma Stone, "…and it's dying, it's dying Mia…but not on my watch." His girlfriend inquired, "What are you going to do?" Sebastian informed that he desired to open his own club where, "We play whatever we want, whenever we want, however we want; as long as it's pure jazz." Inspired by Sebastian's passion, Mia responded positively to him at the onset of dating. She admitted that his commitment to the traditional art form was instrumental in altering her negative view of jazz music, where she began to find appreciation for the craft. At times, Sebastian's allegiance was a vehicle that had the power to influence and welcome others to experience jazz through his loyal lens.

Yet, Sebastian struggled financially and was in need of regular paying work. Though hired to perform specific music (i.e. holiday titles, recent hits, modern jazz), he reluctantly acquiesced in an effort to remain employed. On these occasions when he acceded to the terms of arrangements created with business owners and clients to perform the music of their choice, Sebastian frequently experienced challenges remaining within the boundaries outlined. The detours from the music selections tended to direct him to adding traditional jazz into his performances and sabotaging opportunities to remain employed. In these instances, Sebastian's dedication and loyalty to classic jazz caused him to be uncompromising as a professional, unrelenting to his passion, and unable to experience positive emotion when performing outside of his personal desires. Elshtain, et al. (2013) cited, "loyalty is entangled with faithfulness, endurance, selflessness, generosity, the keeping of promises" (p. 28). Sebastian's loyalty possessed faithfulness, endurance, and promises kept; yet lacked a generosity and selflessness that would allow others to find his loyalty endearing. Consequently, on several occasions, individuals referred to him as a "pain in the ass" to work with. His rigidity also presented with additional repercussions; specifically, his inability to remain employed negatively impacted his ability to sustain his livelihood and build necessary capital to be able to actualize his personal dreams of owning a jazz club.

Furthermore, often Sebastian displayed challenges viewing situations globally and approached life events in a myopic manner. Sebastian's faithful dedication to jazz guided his perception of most situations that he encountered. Additionally, he frequently made life decisions based upon other's appreciation and understanding of jazz music. For example, Sebastian was provided the opportunity to be introduced to a young lady by his sister, Laura, performed by Rosemarie DeWitt. He inquired whether the female liked jazz, anticipating that he might be misunderstood by the individual. When his sister responded that she doubted that she would be interested, Sebastian genuinely inquired, "Then what are we going to talk about?" His response suggested that when jazz was not of interest and a part of moments in his life, there lacked alternative topics worthy of discussion and exploration that might foster a connection between himself and others.

After living with such loyalty and lacking positive gains, his colleague and friend, Keith, acted by John Legend, asked Sebastian to consider performing modern music with a jazz component.

> **KEITH:** I know, it's different. You want to save jazz.
> How gonna save jazz if no one is listening? Jazz is dying
> because of people like you. You playing to 90-year-olds at

the Lighthouse. Where are the kids? Where are the young people? You are so obsessed with Kenny Clark and Thelonious Monk; these guys were revolutionists. How are you gonna be revolutionary if you are such a traditionalist?

Sebastian began to accept that his inflexibility resulted in financial strain and difficulty maintaining steady employment. His living environment coupled with the feeling of being inadequate to provide for his girlfriend and present as a success were further shortcomings experienced by his loyalty and inflexibility. Because performing traditional jazz lacked lucrative options for him, he decided to pursue the opportunity to engage with a band that had a promising financial and successful future. He believed that this job opportunity would yield profits that had the potential to support his dreams of owning a jazz club. Sebastian was aware that the opportunity to perform with the band required compromises of him. In accepting, he would have to agree to minimize his faithfulness to traditional jazz and activate suppressing his desire to play the classics. Further, he would be required to become increasingly selfless and act in the interest of the band, rather than indulge in his personal desires. Doing so would translate to reducing the urge to spontaneously engage in classic jazz. Once beginning to play and experience success, Sebastian appeared committed to the music the band performed. Sebastian's conscious choice to pursue this venture provided him with newfound financial security, however at the sacrifice of pursuing his personal dreams.

At this time, Sebastian was conflicted yet conscious of his options and sacrifices. Does he continue to create music with a successful band and place his dreams of owning a jazz club further on hold, or continue to pursue his dreams and struggle financially? Sebastian was able to articulate that he previously placed effort in pursing the latter option to no avail. He was left holding a decision to make for himself: remain committed to his loyalty and invest in reaching his goals or pursue a level of financial stability and predictability within his life. What shall Sebastian to do?

**What Makes This Character Rich?**

Sebastian presented as a young man with an uncommon level of commitment to his passion. "Loyalty isn't grey. It's black and white. You're either loyal completely, or not loyal at all" (Sharnay, attributed, A-Thousand-Words). And Sebastian was all in. The passionate lens in which he viewed the world, where his musical art was paramount, at times was welcomed and at other times was a sabotaging interloper that impacted his social relations, influenced his self-concept and global reasoning.

Interpersonally, his level of dedication and appreciation caused him to experience difficulty connecting with others in a meaningful way in the absence of jazz. Sebastian presented as fixated and unavailable to be appreciative and gracious of others. When he finds his sister in his home sitting on a bench recovered from the trash, he asked her to remove herself because a famous musician once sat upon it. Further, Sebastian's interest in a gift his sister gave him was only peeked when it was suggested that Miles Davis once urinated upon it. Such behaviors of having narrow interests and minimal tolerance of topics outside of one's personal activities significantly hinder one's availability to engage in positive interactions with others.

Reaching adulthood includes individuals whom are ready of "accepting responsibility for oneself, making independent decisions, and becoming financially independent" (Arnett, 2007, p. 69). Sebastian was presented with opportunities that caused him to make challenging decisions. He noted that he was "growing up" and that process required him to decide where his dedication to jazz belonged in his life. Sebastian began to determine whether he could afford to continue allowing his loyalty to jazz be a deciding factor in whether he accepted employment, pursued dating a specific individual, or engaged in the world in a productive way. He contemplated whether jazz could continue to dictate his overall view of his environment and how he navigated the world. With such decisions hanging in the balance, Sebastian's loyalty to jazz, which defined this character as a "serious musician," also amounted to the need to reassess his belief in his self-identity.

Because many of Sebastian's thoughts focused upon jazz, as mentioned earlier, he approached most situations with narrow attention. Not until he met his girlfriend Mia, performed by Emma Stone, was he able to conceptualize bifurcating his loyalty between two interests. "Compassionate love is the more encompassing construct because it includes tenderness, caring and other aspects of empathy, but also behavioral predispositions such as self-sacrifice" (Sprecher & Fehr, 2005, p. 630). Subsequently, he learned by loving Mia that he could be loyal to jazz and have loyalty for another. He could receive unconditional support to follow his dreams, and he could support another's interest(s) with an equal level of commitment as he had invested in jazz. Sebastian's realization was illustrated as he drove to find Mia once she returned to her hometown, broken by failure, and encouraged her to continue to have faith in her talents.

Sebastian was initially witnessed believing that he would be unable to split his loyalty for jazz with anything or with anyone. Once meeting Mia, he began to feel a "rat, tat, tat" in his heart that made him "want to stay," in the relationship as noted in the song "City of Stars" (performed by Sebastian and Mia, music by

Justin Hurwitz, lyrics by Pasek & Paul). His faithfulness to jazz at times negatively impacted his perceptions and behaviors yet made him a magnetic character due to his level of expressed loyalty. Sebastian's ability to manage his passions and strike a balance between preserving his strong interest that contributed to his self-concept was instrumental in the illustration of this character. In the end, his increased flexibility allowed him to become receptive to handle situations in a new productive way that brought upon his desired success.

BEST PSYCHOLOGY IN FILM

## *MIA*

Performed by: Emma Stone

*SELF-DOUBT*

> *"The brick walls are there for a reason. The brick walls are not there to keep us out. The brick walls are there to give us a chance to show how badly we want something. Because the brick walls are there to stop the people who don't want it badly enough. They're there to stop the other people."*
>
> – Randy Rausch

Having a dream for one's career is a long-term commitment. Nurturing aspirations require persistence, continued dedication, and resilience. Further, one's personal abilities and talents must lend themselves to what is necessary to be successful. Actualizing is a process; and the journey towards meeting one's goals tend to be filled with successes and failures. When failures are met more frequently than successes, one may begin to wonder whether the dream they have has the possibility to come true. Mia, performed by Emma Stone, finds her efforts dimly recognized, which caused her confidence to diminish and self-doubt to augment. Despite rejections, Mia continued to audition to show her talents in an effort to finally obtain the recognition she desired to become a professional actress.

"By definition, self-doubtful individuals are uncertain whether their ability alone can produce a success" (Braslow, et.al., 2012, p. 476). Mia, an aspiring actress presented as a determined individual, dedicated to becoming a professional. To remain close to her passion, she became employed in a coffee shop as a barista upon the Warner Brothers lot to surround herself by the craft and those who were gainfully employed in the industry. Her love of film and desire to become an actress led her to remain invested in auditioning for television shows and films. Audition after audition resulted in others being cast, which directly began to take a toll on her self-esteem and self-confidence. She described, "there's people in the waiting room that's like me; and, but prettier and better and at; and maybe I'm not good enough."

Once experiencing multiple rejections, individuals may question one's talents. In fact, "most people doubt their ability at times" (Carroll, et.al., 2011, p. 190). As Carroll et al. (2011) suggests, "ironically, then, self-uncertainty, or doubt, may be one of the few certainties left in modern life" (p. 190). However, "no one flourishes if they are constantly being told they are not good enough, whether that voice comes from inside or out" (Wright, 2004, p. 29). Eleanor Roosevelt stated, "the future belongs to those who believe in the beauty of their dreams." Once an individual feels rejected frequently, continued belief in oneself feels futile and the outside voices of being rejected can become internalized and a constant voice in mind.

Mia's questions regarding her abilities and whether her talents would manifest into a career arrived once her auditions did not lead to roles. Yet, self-doubt can occur at any time, prior to attempts to gain success and once action has occurred that have been met with failure. Despite when self-doubt occurs, "individuals who experience self-doubt may overly focus on perceived imperfections and their fear of failure" (Peer & McAuslan, 2015, p. 176).

Possessing a dream can create a specific vision of what life will look like when actualized. When one has not reached their goals and desired self, self-doubt manifests "primarily from the presence of a strong undesired self of prospective failure in awareness" (Carroll, et.al., 2011, p. 190). Once self-doubt is experienced, it can be challenging for these feelings to dissipate; rather, one can begin to question "about their competence and routinely feel distressed about upcoming performance" (Zhao & Wichman, 2015, p. 1), as illustrated below:

**SEBASTIAN:** "She wants you to audition for this huge movie that she's got."

**MIA:** "I'm not going to that. I'm not going to that."

**SEBASTIAN:** "What?"

**MIA:** "That one is going to be. No, that one's going to be."

**SEBASTIAN:** "I'm sorry?"

**MIA:** "That will kill me."

"Uncertainty about one's ability in performance situations suggests the prospect of failure and can prompt defensive, protective behavior" (Hermann, et al., 2008, p. 395). Mia found that once her desired self felt distant from her actual existence despite her efforts, self-doubt ensued. These feelings caused her to become defensive and use both avoidance and withdrawal as a way to defend against her fears.

**SEBASTIAN:** "Why don't you want to do it anymore?"

**MIA:** "Because, I think that it hurts a little too much."

Consequently, when new opportunities arose, she shared with Sebastian the hesitance she possessed and desire to withdraw from placing efforts towards auditioning, even for a lead role crafted for her. Her self-doubt coupled with the fear of experiencing additional failure grew to avoidance in an effort to protect her remaining self-esteem. Individuals who have high levels of self-doubt "spend inordinate amounts of time dwelling on their competence shortcomings" (Hermann, et al., 2008, p. 406). During the moment that Mia was encouraged to continue to seek her dream, she questioned her level of competence and wondered whether she would be, in fact, "good enough."

Once self-doubt materializes, one can choose to continue to experience this emotion or find techniques to cope and manage its effects. "People strive specifically to cope with feelings of self-doubt about their competence, sometimes striving to reduce their uncertainties" (Braslow, et.al., 2012, p. 471). Individuals may solicit the use of internal services such as self-handicapping where one may "undermine one's own performance to obscure the link between ability and performance" and use overachieving where one expends "an extraordinary amount of effort to achieve high performance" (Zhao & Wichman, 2015, p. 2). Being able to recognize and understand the effects of self-doubt on one's view of self and performance can enable the use of systems that assist in being better able to move past self-doubts and into one's desired future.

**What Makes This Character Rich?**

Mia is a character that is easily relatable. In her mid-twenties, she has a career dream and the drive to make her future what she desires for herself. As with many, her dreams of becoming an actress are not easily obtainable. She must possess a stamina, persistence and resilience for criticism and rejection to ultimately arrive at success. She faced many unsuccessful encounters, yet exhibited an unwavering dedication to her craft. When self-doubt entered her experience, "the destructive inner critic had taken over her consciousness, and when we hear a voice telling us we are rubbish all the time, it stops us seeing things clearly" (Wright, 2014, p. 29). In the midst of ultimate defeat, she began to believe that her hopes were ill founded. This self-doubt motivated Mia to return to her parent's home in Bolder City, Nevada to re-group and potentially change her goals, and thus the trajectory of her life.

**MIA:** "It's over."

**SEBASTIAN:** "What is?"

**MIA:** "It's over."

**SEBASTIAN:** "What?"

**MIA:** "All of this. I'm done embarrassing myself. I'm done, I'm done. Nobody showed up."

**SEBASTIAN:** "So what?"

**MIA:** "I can't pay back the theater. I'm going home."

Dissimilar to many characters, the audience is not provided an opportunity to witness the defense mechanisms that Mia utilized to assist her in moving through self-doubts and into the audition that was a life-changing role. What was illustrated included the magnitude and well-entrenched nature of her self-doubt at the time that caused her to pause to continue to pursue her life dream. Fortunately, as she wavered, she was able to rely upon the support and faith of her boyfriend to sustain and propel her advancement.

"If we allow ourselves to be subjected to the relentless attack of the inner critic, we block out the capacity of our hearts to express compassion for ourselves" (Wright, 2014, p. 29). Relying upon the determination of others when one is unable to independently muster the energy and efforts to hold a positive self-belief highlights the beneficial healing impact of emotional support. Being receptive to support "is an acknowledgement that while we may mess up, we are equally deserving of respect and compassion" (Wright, 2014, p. 29). As a result, it is not always effortless for individuals to access positive feelings about one's capabilities, especially when injured and doubtful.

Having a strong emotional support network lends itself to having individuals who can be called upon in times of self-doubt. Possessing such a network where people believe unconditionally in one's talents creates an environment where "even transitory feelings of self-doubt about one's competence are not likely to stand unchallenged" (Braslow, et.al., 2012, p. 475). Mia's emotional support was delivered by Sebastian encouraging her to be willing to risk being vulnerable one additional time and audition for a part that he believed would yield positive results.

**SEBASTIAN:** "How's the play going?"

**MIA:** "Umm, I'm nervous."

**SEBASTIAN:** "You are?"

**MIA:** "Umm hum."

**SEBASTIAN:** "Why?"

**MIA:** "Because. What if people show up?"

**SEBASTIAN:** "Pishicocka. You're nervous about what they think?"

**MIA:** "I'm nervous to do it. I'm nervous to get up on a stage and perform for people. But I don't need to say that to you."

**SEBASTIAN:** "It's going to be incredible."

**MIA:** "I'm terrified."

**SEBASTIAN:** "They should be so lucky to see you. I can't wait."

**MIA:** "I can."

Self-doubt, "a feeling of doubt about one's own abilities or actions" (Merriam-Webster Dictionary, 2017) is not entirely an unhealthy emotion. Braslow (2012) described that a healthy dose of self-doubt is a "wise medicine" (p. 471). This emotion does not have to be debilitating for individuals; rather, it facilitates humility (Verducci, 2014) and fosters questions regarding one's performance. This emotion can be an influential agent to drive motivation to refine skills and increase competence. Additionally, when one experiences self-doubt, it can also elicit the identification of those in one's personal network who are able to provide unconditional support and believe in one's talents, even during times when one is unable to believe in oneself. According to Roy T. Bennett, (2016), "Dreams don't work unless you take action. The surest way to make your dreams come true is to live them." Mia's confidence in herself and during difficult times, her faith in Sebastian's belief in her abilities allowed her to regain fortitude that empowered her to believe that "all our dreams can come true, if we have the courage to pursue them" (Walt Disney).

BEST PSYCHOLOGY IN FILM

## *LION*

Directed by: Garth Davis

## *SCENE I*

*Saroo runs upon a dirt terrain. He stands amidst hundreds of butterflies with his arms open and suddenly lifted. His brother, Guddu yells for him. Guddu jumps onto a moving train.*

**GUDDU:** "Come on. Come on! Get up! Come on. Quickly. Hold it properly."

*Guddu stoops atop of a train car full with coal. Saroo grasps the side of the train car opening a satchel.*

**GUDDU:** "Saroo, catch!"
**GUARD:** "Get down!"
**SAROO:** "Guddu! The guards!"
**GUARD:** "Hey, boy, get down! Go! Get down, boy!"

*Guddu stands upon the mound of coal. The train enters a tunnel. Saroo screams."*

**SAROO:** "Guddu!"

BEST PSYCHOLOGY IN FILM

*ADOPTING*

> *"What makes a family is neither the absence of tragedy nor the ability to hide from misfortune, but the courage to overcome it and, from that broken past, write a new beginning."*
>
> – Steve Pemberton,
>
> *A Chance in the World: An Orphan Boy, a Mysterious Past, and How He Found a Place Called Home*

There are many ways to adopt; through the foster care system, a stepchild where the "stepparent typically adopts the biological child of the spouse he or she is marrying" and when a "heterosexual married couple, unrelated to a child, who wishes to adopt, usually because of infertility" (Grotevant, et al, 2000, p. 380). Before continuing, recognized family dynamics have changed over the years. Same-sex couples readily adopt and provide nurturing homes to children in need of care. Single, non-married individuals pursue adopting one to many children originating from a single household to children all around the world. It is attempted in this writing to honor the diversity found in families. These attempts are accomplished by widening the vocabulary to address "adoptive parents" rather than solely "mothers". Direct quotes and research offering data that assessed adoptive mothers tender useful findings, yet may impede these efforts. However, I am hopeful that the spirit of inclusion can be held when proceeding.

"Adoption occurs in all societies" (March, 1995, p. 653). Despite where adoption occurs and with whom, there are specific participants consistently involved that includes the adoptee, the adoptive parent, and the family of origin. Lifton (2010) described that "the story of adoption is a ghost story, full of fantasy, mystery, and missing persons, who, for the most part, are 'as if' dead, unlike respectable ghosts, who are unambiguously dead" (p. 71) affect each participant of the adoption process. For the adoptee, "the ghost of the golden child his adoptive parents might have had" (p. 71) looms as a concern regarding who he/she is within the present and who he/she will become in the future. "He is also accompanied by the ghost of the original baby he was before being adopted-the child he might have been had he stayed with his birth mother" (p. 71). For the biological mother, "the ghost of the adoptive parents hover about. She feels ambivalent towards them: both grateful and resentful" (p. 72). And she "carries the ghost of the baby she relinquished, who like her trauma remains frozen in time" (p. 72). Lastly, for the adoptive parents "ghosts encountered here represent lost babies, the parents who lost them, and the parents who found them" (p. 71). How individuals in the adoptive triad emotionally processes adoption evolves over time. In the film *Lion*, directed by Garth Davis, the audience is provided an illustration of the experience of the Brierley family (based upon a true story), and how they navigated and managed intercountry adoption. *Lion* provides an inside view of the journey all participants took to create resolution and peace surrounding the adoption experience.

"How do adoptees come to terms with being adopted" (Reinosa, et al., 2013, p. 264) into a home? The understanding of adoption tends to change gradually throughout time, where different factors become important as the adoptee matures. As young children learn regarding what adoption means and begin to conceptualize its institution, adoptees may "start to recognize that adoption implies not just building a family (their adoptive family) but also losing a family (their birth family)" (Reinosa, et al., 2013, pp. 264-265). During "this developmental stage, they may experience a profound sense of loss and difference with regards to others" (Reinosa, et al., 2013, p. 265).

Also, amongst their peers, children may feel the presence of "social discrimination from others who questioned their rightful position within the adoptive family structure" (March, 1995, p. 654) when they confide in others regarding their history. As children age and enter preteen and teenager stages, the desire to be similar to peers increases. At this age, and adoptees in particular, "have a keen awareness of reactions from others that characterized them as different from the norm," according to March (1995, p. 659), where they perceive their adoption is likely to be viewed as a social stigma. Adoptees have noted fear when others learn they were adopted; the listener never believes that the adopted parents would ever love them as much as they may have loved their biological child. Adoptees note that people have "questioned the strength of their adoptive parent-child bonds and their position within the adoptive family structure" (March, 1995, p. 656-657). Of concern, adopted children may begin to "harbor negative images of the self" (Grotevant, et al, 2000, p. 379). Further, "an adopted child's sense of worth may be affected by certain disclosures about his or her birthparents or their circumstances, and require that the child attempt to reconcile an emerging sense of morality" (Grotevant, et al., 2000, p. 379). These felt stigmas can be experienced both externally and internally. The adoptee can become inclined to have a need to defend their fantasized biological family's behaviors. Equally, they may defend the adoptive parents love for them as a result of other's believed perceptions of their life's narrative. During this time, the adoptee may experience the negative influence of these stigmas on their self-image that in turn impacts their feelings of self-worth. In an effort to safeguard the adoptee, "adoptive parents are encouraged to develop strategies to approach their children about their background and culture of origin" (Lindgren & Zetterqvist Nelson, 2014, p. 540).

Within *Lion*, the protagonist, Saroo (performed by Dev Patel), was a youngster when his adoptive parents adopted him. From birth until the age of five, he engaged in positive relations with his family of origin. Yet, due to becoming lost and unable to find his way home, he endured months of homelessness. Eventually, Saroo was placed in an orphanage, and finally adopted to a loving family, the Brierley's, in Tasmania, Australia. Being adopted from a different country and relocating to the country of adoptive parents created numerous dynamics. Issues of diversity become present and in the foreground, as the adoptee—regardless of attire, haircuts, and other modifications—will tend to look different from their adoptive parents (Reinosa, et al., 2013). These "children have been adopted into a family of different race (transracial adoption) and have a different physical appearance and cultural heritage compared with their adopted parents" (Reinosa, et al., 2013, p. 265). Literature, as described below, suggests that as the adoptee matures into teenage years, increased interest in their family of origin surfaces.

## CURIOSITY

Historically, many countries that permitted intercountry adoptions made searching for biological families a restriction. Adopting from other countries lent to the idea that once adopted, there was "a clean break from the old life and a new start in a new world" (Lindgren & Zetterqvist Nelson, 2014, p. 541). However, "for adopted persons, a unique focus of curiosity is their own adoption" (Wrobel, et al., 2013, p. 441). Adoptees have "needs [that] propel people into relationships with their birth" (Howe & Feast, 2001, p. 363) parent and express "the need and desire to know their biological origins" (Grotevant, et al, 2000, p. 381). Though for some adoptees, "being born in another country has never been an issue" for other adoptees there is a sadness, a "sorrow of not knowing what an alternative life would have been like" (Lindgren& Zetterqvist Nelson, 2014, pp. 545 & 547). "For persons who were adopted, this question adds layers of anxiety because they have different parents of birth and rearing and because knowledge of their biological heritage may be incomplete" (Grotevant, et al, 2000, p. 379). "The wish to have these questions answered explains why so many adopted people feel the need to search for and have contact with their birth mother" (Howe & Feast, 2001, p. 363). As a result of such feelings, some adoptees begin to articulate that searching for their birth parent becomes a strong desire and begins to hold great importance (Grotevant, et al, 2000).

"Research has drawn attention to the fact that for most adopted people, although not all, there is a curiosity about discovering their origins which emerges into an active and often prolonged journey in search of birth family" (Winter & Cohen, 2005, p. 46-47). As this phase may be difficult for the adoptee, it can be equally "difficult for the adoptive parents too" (Reinosa, et al., 2013, p. 265). Although "adopters anticipated that their child would need and seek more information from their birth family as they progressed through their teenage years" (MacDonald & McSherry, 2011, p. 9), they can struggle to hold in mind that the quest to locate the biological family is not indicative of whether the adoptee experienced a negative or positive adoption experience (Winter & Cohen, 2005). For some adopters, there is a "phenomenon of psychological presence" "with the birth family featuring regularly in their thinking, even where there was little or no actual contact with them" (MacDonald & McSherry, 2011, p. 13). This can generate anxiety in adopters regarding their child's curiosity to further investigate regarding their birth origins. However, most adoptive parents grow less uneasy once learning that feeling curious regarding one's family and country of origin is a common experience for adoptees. In fact, "increasing numbers of adult adopted people are searching for and having reunions with their birth relatives" (Howe & Feast, 2001, p. 351). In response to curious feelings, it fuels the adoptee with "the motivation to engage in information-seeking behavior" (Wrobel, et al., 2013, p. 441). "The perception that adoption entails severe emotional loss that must be resolved has is now so prevalent that adoptees are often expected to try to find their birth parents" (Wang, et al., 2015, p. 48).

Though questions regarding the family and place of origin are a typical part of the development process for adoptees, "one should never press adoptees to search; they may not be ready" (Lifton, 2010, p. 74).

> Some adopted persons display no desire to seek out such information, whereas others feel so curious that they will use multiple avenues to find out what they want to know and will not stop their efforts until they get answers (Wrobel, et al., 2013, p. 441).

"When this happens, adoptees embark on what is known as The Search" (Lifton, 2010, p. 74).

**THE SEARCH**

Grotevant, et al. (2000) noted that the desire to search for one's family of origin can be influenced by "the journey of identity development," which he described as "complex and potentially problematic for adopted persons" (p.

382). He continued, "we can think of adoptive identity as involving three levels: an intrapsychic component, a component involving relationships with the family, and a component involving the social world beyond the family" that "connects personality, subjective awareness, relationships and external context" (p. 380). Grotevant, et al. (2000) hypothesized that the "intense curiosity some adopted persons may have about their biological heritage and birthparents" may be an effort "to synthesize their dual identities" (p. 382). However, for many adoptee and intercountry adoptees, the search for one's parent(s) of origin is challenging and faced with various barriers.

Barriers can represent both internal and external causes (Wrobel, et al., 2013). Internally, the desire to actualize moving forward to locate the place of origin and biological family can cause adoptees to begin to experience fears that "they could lose their adoptive parents, who might feel betrayed" (Lifton, 2010, p. 74) by their searching behaviors. Externally, "barriers can also include people, policies and resources" where "encountering barriers can produce frustration that can enhance or diminish curiosity" (Wrobel, et al., 2013, p. 442). As a result, "most searches unfolded in stages spread over several years, involving many false starts and stops" (Wang, et al., 2015, p. 63). Further, searching can "be quite expensive depending on the circumstances, such as whether parents decided to hire local searchers or make repeated visits" (Wang, et al., 2015, p. 63) to countries to locate additional information. Individuals who are adopted "can be grouped under four themes: who searches; why they search; what they are searching for; and, finally, the outcomes of the search process" (Winter & Cohen, 2005, p. 46). These factors can help sustain motivation for adoptees to continue when they encounter difficulties that reduce hope and give the impression that the search is no longer worth pursuing. Yet, research has found that "barriers increased curiosity, which in turn increased information-seeking" (Wrobel, et al., 2013, p. 448). Data support how "an increasing number of adoptees, after much ambivalence and delay, take the risk and cross over" (Lifton, 2010, p. 74) to begin the process of finding information regarding their birth despite challenges experienced.

The decision to begin the search for one's place of birth and birth parent(s) is not an independent decision. Fantasies of what steps will occur once information is found can follow. Whether one will initiate a reunion suddenly becomes a realistic opportunity.

> While early debates about contact focused on whether it was good or bad overall for the child, the finding that it is not necessarily either, but dependent upon myriad variables specific to the individual child and context, has led to more subtle questions being asked about the factors that might ensure that contact will be experienced beneficially (MacDonald & McSherry, 2011, p. 5).

Upon locating an adoptee's biological family, a new understanding of the world in which they could have lived in forms. Novel ideas regarding the world in which they have lived their lives in are also created. Adoptees describe in comparable ways how visiting their birth country made them think about how their lives could have been. They describe a sense of seeing parallel life-course trajectories, and their narratives stress how arbitrary accidental occurrences shape one's life trajectory (Lindgren & Zetterqvist Nelson, 2014, p. 547).

**REUNION**

"Although there is an established literature on adopted people who search for their birth relatives, little is known about the actual experience of contact and reunion" (Howe & Feast, 2001, p. 351). "Unlike most media representations that portray such occasions as exclusively joyful and happy, most participants claimed that their initial meetings produced a perplexing mixture of positive and negative feelings" (Wang, et al., 2015, p. 55-56). However, many adoptees who have participated in a reunion have experienced significant benefits in meeting their biological families. Adoptees have described that they "were gratified to observe physical similarities between" themselves "and their birth relatives and to have clarified aspects of" (Wang, et al., 2015, p. 63) their histories. The more information that the adoptee was able to obtain from their family of origin regarding their background, the greater the satisfaction the adoptee felt from the reunion process (March, 1995).

Additionally, "research has also highlighted the emotional and psychological benefits to most (but not all) adopted people of re-establishing these connections" (Winter & Cohen, 2005, p. 45). Specifically, the reunion can provide adoptees with a sense of being accepted socially by the information they discover (March, 1995). As adoptees may feel that others stigmatize adoption, the reunion can help adoptees acquire "information to respond more appropriately to others' questions, they became more comfortable with their adoptive status" (March, 1995, p. 658). Further, the reunion helps "answer questions about origin, background, and the reasons for being placed" (Howe & Feast, 2001, p. 362). Adoptees are increasingly inclined to feel "they have gained more power over their presentation of self and over negative assumptions that others might make about their biological history and the reasons for their adoption" (March, 1995, p. 658).

"Whatever the outcome of adopted people's reunion with their birth relative, most said the search and contact experience had been satisfying and worthwhile" (Howe & Feast, 2001, p. 362). Making contact with biological family members allowed adoptees to answer unknown mysteries of their history while satisfying the basic desire of "see[ing] someone to whom they were biologically related and who might well look like them" (Howe & Feast, 2001, p. 362). Most adoptees, when asked, feel that the reunion was a positive experience; and, as a result, many chose to remain in contact with their birth family. Adoptive parents who fear that adoptees will gravitate to their biological parents and cease contact; though adoptees may remain in contact with their family of origin, the number who remain in contact with their adoptive families remain higher where they are more likely to remain in contact with the adoptive mother over time (Howe & Feast, 2001). Adoptees "say that they had learned to appreciate their adoptive family more since the reunion" and "their primary relationship was still with their adoptive mother, even in those cases where a long-term relationship had been established with her birth mother" (Howe & Feast, 2001, p. 358-364). Adoptive parents learn that "they are still the parents, just not the exclusive ones. They will learn that they can not lose their child." (Lifton, B.J., 2010, p. 75).

All reunions do not end in roses and sunshine. For some adoptees, contact with their 'birth mother' was met with "mixed or negative feelings" that encouraged adoptees to "cease contact with their birth mother" (Howe & Feast, 2001, p. 364). "When the adoption information known matches the information desired, there is no information gap and no curiosity" (Wrobel, et al., 2013, p. 442), which can motivate discontinuing the desire to create a relationship with the birth parent. Once the adoptee's curiosity is quenched and/or the contact with the biological family does not offer desired positive emotions, additional contact may no longer feel necessary.

"Coinciding with an increase in the use of adoption for children in care, the past 30 years have seen a steady move away from secrecy towards open communication with the adopted child about their adoption" (MacDonald & McSherry, 2011, p. 4). The ghost story Lifton offers to describe adoption that illustrates "trauma, unresolved grief, dissociation and regression, much of which everyone in the adoption triad experiences" (2010, p. 71) highlights the gravity the adoption experience has upon the adopter, adoptee, and the birth parent(s). Further, because "the diversity of adoptive parents and children being adopted is increasing" it creates "complex contexts for adoptive identity development in which differences are heightened within families and between the family and the community" (Grotevant, et al, 2000, p. 380). Stigmas surrounding adoption can be experienced by the adoptee; where, as a consequence, adoption is "returned to, consciously and unconsciously, at various points in an adoptee's development" (Reinosa, et al., 2013, p. 264) prior to finding a feeling of resolution. What results is a "curiosity [that] provides the motivation" to seek for information and a possible reunion with the birth parent(s) (Wrobel, et al., 2013, p. 442).

Today, "it is unclear how many adoptive families agree to and maintain contact" (MacDonald & McSherry, 2011, p. 6) once a reunion occurs. And "it is impossible to foresee how individual adoptees will understand and deal with their background" (Lindgren & Zetterqvist Nelson, 2014, p. 542). However, understanding that the emotional process of adoption can be a lengthy voyage, one that exists over the lifespan, assists in coping with the brevity of this experience for all within the adoption triad.

BEST PSYCHOLOGY IN FILM

## *SAROO*

Performed by Dev Patel

*INTEGRATING*

## BEST PSYCHOLOGY IN FILM

> *"Adoption is a lifelong journey. It means different things to me at different times. Sometimes it is just a part of who I am. Other times it is something I am actively going through."*
>
> – Kelly DiBenedetto, *Adoption Is a Lifelong Journey*

Within the pages exploring the film, *Lion*, theories are discussed regarding how adoptees navigate the journey of reconciling their adoption with their family of origin, adoptive family, and within themselves. The portrayal of Saroo, acted by Dev Patel, illustrates one boy's experience of being lost, adopted, and maturing into an emerging adult. Within his development, he experienced what theorists propose occurs: curiosity, The Search and Reunion with his family of origin. Saroo's experience is a demonstration of a persistent passionate pursuit that one can take to discover one's past to inform one's present self.

Once lost, Saroo found himself many months as a five-year-old living independently and homeless. In essence, Saroo became a child living on the streets of Calcutta, India. "Life on the street is defined by a continuous struggle to survive, physically and psychologically" (Schimmel, 2008, p. 215). During this time, Saroo faced challenging times where he struggled to successfully interface with adults due to proven untrustworthiness. For examples, Saroo successfully escaped adults who preyed upon children huddled in tunnels for shelter for unexplained purposes. As the children scurried and screamed in terror, the worst was left for the audience to imagine. Saroo soon connected with an adult woman who welcomed him into her home. She appeared willing to offer safety, yet was suddenly found to be crafty and devious. She bathed and clothed Saroo and allowed him to drink soda, though arranged for him to be trafficked to a known man in search for boys such as he. "One of the most developmentally and psychologically significant deprivations that street children face is a lack of the experience of unconditional positive regard, of love and of a supportive and emotionally intimate relationship with an adult" (Schimmel, 2008, p. 214). Saroo quickly learned that adults who appeared caring could not be trusted. As his suspicions grew due to his keen intuition, Saroo escaped the home, running for his life. Schimmel (2008) continued that "children need a source of sustained emotional support" and "the dependable, consistent and intense love and nurturing that most children are accustomed to receiving from their parents are conspicuously absent" (pp. 215-216). For Saroo, once losing his family on a typical night from a nearby city from his home in Ganesh Talai, India, his ability to receive care and attention from trusting loving adults significantly diminished.

Once adopted, the instability Saroo experienced dissipated. He was adopted into a loving home and provided consistent safety and love. Years thereafter, as an emerging adult, Saroo performed well. He possessed career goals that involved entering the field of hotel management and hospitality. He appeared secure and well accustomed to his life in Australia. Saroo, as many adoptees, was "generally satisfied with their adoptive family" (Reinosa, et al., 2013, p. 271).

Relocating to a nearby city for studies, Saroo was introduced to his cohort of peers. Naturally, questions arose to learn more about one another. "Everyone has seen the shrug and heard the line: 'Adoption means nothing to me'" (Lifton, 2010, pp. 74-76). "According to this line of thought, as the child gained experiences of her or his new cultural context and adapted to it, s/he would leave her/his 'old' culture behind and become" a participant in their adoptive family's home country (Lind, 2011, p. 120). When Saroo's peers inquired regarding his history and ethnicity, his response of, "I'm adopted, I'm not really Indian," raised eyebrows. "This statement signals the splitting off that has taken place from an early age" (Lifton, 2010, p. 76) for some adoptees where they unconsciously lose awareness of their identity prior to adoption.

"International/transracial adoption, in which children's different physical appearance often makes their adoptive status visible and obvious" (Reinosa, et al., 2013, p. 270) suggests that a dissociation process would be more challenging to accomplish. Not only would one view themselves daily and recognize varied attributes of those around them; but, others could equally hold in mind such differences. However, Saroo was able to successfully "split off" (Lifton, 2010, p. 76) his birthplace from his identity. Atypically, Saroo was unable to identify with his racial and ethnic grouping where most adoptees, when inquired, "correctly identified with their own racial group", is "conscious of their own physical and racial features" and "international adoptees mainly identified themselves as being from their birth country" (Reinosa, et al., 2013, p. 270). Reinosa and colleagues (2013) also found that dissimilar to Saroo, who resided in his place of birth for five years, "most adoptees had not visited their birth country" (p. 270). Despite the lack of exposure, "adopted young children tend to identify racially ethnically with their birth culture" (p. 270) and "appear to develop a stronger sense of cultural identity with the birth country" (p. 271).

When transitions occur and "after some major event in their lives-marriage, the birth of a child, losing a job, the death of an adoptive parent" one can begin to reexamine one's past and upbringing. After relocating and meeting curious peers, Saroo was challenged to begin to reconcile his past with his present. "Mental images he had created of what it would be like were actual memories" of his family interactions (Lindgren & Zetterqvist Nelson, 2014, p. 550). Saroo described, "I'm lost," which sparked the curiosity that Howe & Feast (2001), Lindgren & Zetterqvist Nelson (2014), Grotevant, et al. (2000), MacDonald & McSherry (2011), and Reinosa, et al. (2013), amongst others mention. Similar to these theorists' findings, Saroo suddenly had a desire to locate both his home of origin and his identity.

"Adoptees are vulnerable during this period, for they often feel they have no self at all" (Lifton, 2010, p. 78); and, consequently, "as children grow older, integrating an adoptive identity may require more information than is available, and the desire to visit their birth country may then arise" (Reinosa, et al., 2013, p. 270). Additionally, "adoptees placed as older children had direct experience with their birth families prior to their adoption and may wonder how birth relatives are currently faring" (Wrobel, et al., 2013, p. 442). As the memories of his birth family began to flood his daily experience, Saroo suddenly became engrossed with the possibility of relocating his birth family and his investigation became paramount to him.

For numerous adoptees, "the birth mother became the object of their search" (March, 1995, p. 654). For Saroo, his biological mother, (acted by Priyanka Bose), and beloved brother, Guddu, performed by Abhishek Bharate, were the objects he desired to reconnect with. Successfully finding his birth home via maps found upon the Internet, the possibility to reunite with his biological family became a reality. Saroo believed that connecting could offer him "the possibility of gaining unlimited access to background information about the biological family" (March, 1995, p. 657).

Embarking upon the actual voyage, flying to another continent to find the family that he lost, Saroo appeared to have a calmness and gentle anticipation. Lifton (2010) suggested that,

> No matter how prepared they think they are, they discover that reunion is an extreme experience, connecting them not only to the joy of knowing their birth family, but to the trauma of the separation that took place, with its feelings of unresolved grief and abandonment (p. 74).

"Regardless of where they take place, reunions are extremely emotional, unpredictable events" (Wang, et al., 2015, p. 55).

Similar to current findings, upon reuniting, Saroo's experience was an emotional reconnection that contained feelings of disappointment initially; yet filled with relief, love, joy, and grief. He was able to gain answers to the questions he held regarding is family of origin. He discovered what hindered his brother from returning to the train platform bench where he slept awaiting his return. He was able to learn regarding his mother's search when he became lost. He uncovered that his biological mother held hope to reunite with him by never leaving the village where they once lived as a family. Additionally, Saroo was also able to reconnect with his now adult sister.

Howe & Feast (2001) found within their study of adoptees in London that once reuniting with the family of origin, "88 percent of adopted people rated the contact with their birth mother as positive" (p. 357) and "eighty-four percent of adopted people said the reunion had helped answer important questions about themselves and their adoption" (p. 357). Further, "63 percent of adopted people who had actually met their birth mother were still in some form of contact with her" (p. 362). Saroo's adoptive parents, in complete support of his journey, lacked a feeling of being "threatened by their child's need to know about his birth mother, and even to meet her eventually" (Lifton, 2010, p. 78). As a result, Saroo's voyage with the support of loved ones allowed him to arrive at conclusions that were imperative for his continued development and progression through life.

**What Makes This Character Rich?**

Defensively, Lifton (2010) noted that adoptees tend to access the use of dissociation to manage and cope with feelings around being adopted. Dissociation is defined by Gabbard (2005) as the disruption of "one's sense of continuity in the areas of identity, memory, consciousness, or perception as a way of retaining an illusion of psychological control in the face of helplessness and loss of control" (p. 35). Dissociation helped enable Saroo to navigate his current life in the absence of emotional conflict and a lack of conscious awareness of the complexities that surrounded his adoption. The use of this defense also fostered his ability to function successfully within his daily life in the absence of anxieties and known internal conflict. Lifton (2010) noted that, "when their dissociation lifts, and they [adoptees] have access to their psychological need to reconnect with the past and know where they came from" (p. 74) they are inclined to participate in The Search to locate their family of origin. Saroo found that as he aged he lost his ability to connect culturally with his home of origin, India. "For in order to survive in the family in which they mysteriously find themselves, adoptees dissociate-split off the self that might have been" (Lifton, B.J., 2010, p. 72). Saroo may have used this defensive strategy to assimilate and accommodate within his new life in a foreign country and new home. Once Saroo entered an emotional space in which he was primed to explore new ideas, thoughts and experiences (professional school), his history slowly became within conscious awareness. Soon, Saroo began to "visit in their [his] daydreams and spin out myriad fantasies-both positive and negative-about the life they [he] might have had" (Lifton, 2010, p. 72).

Interpersonally, connecting immediately with inquisitive and supportive mates, Saroo was surrounded by individuals who were willing to assist him in searching for his family of origin. They readily suggested strategies and technology he could use to locate his birthplace. Parents tend "to be the most important figures with whom to talk about the adoption" (Reinosa, et al., 2013, p. 271). And, though prior to Saroo's desire to find his biological family this dynamic was true for him, once he desired to pursue searching for his biological parents, he struggled to connect—even with his adoptive parents. His girlfriend confronted him and asked why he could not share with his adoptive parents "what you have been up to". Saroo demanded that she not make additional comments regarding his process. As he became deeper into the search, Saroo's images of his brother, mother, and travels to his village became clearer and his interactions with others in his present life became less intimate. Avoiding visits from his adoptive father and worrying that "it will kill her (his adoptive mother) if she knew I was searching" invited Saroo to rationalize remaining distant from his loved ones.

Thereafter, his quest to find answers to his past and build his identity began to consume Saroo. His adaptive functioning of grooming and sleeping became increasingly compromised by his preoccupations. He continued to limit his communication with the caring individuals in his life, was unable to connect with his girlfriend and noted that "and we just went about in our privileged lives, it makes me sick. I have to find her. They need to know I'm okay." Empathizing that his process of identity exploration was essential to his emotional wellbeing, his girlfriend reassured him when he asked for her to wait for him responded, "I'm here." To prepare for his journey, he returned to his primary support; his adoptive family. Sharing his search and efforts to locate his birthplace, his adoptive mother expressed relief in being able to become privy to his journey stating, "So this is where you've been."

The power of finding one's past is a powerful, transformative experience. Saroo discovered that he could develop ways to integrate his past with his present and future. Specifically, he found that "the restored relationship does not necessarily invalidate or dilute the affectional bonds formed with the adoptive parents" (Howe & Feast, 2001, p. 365). Rather,

> the adopted parent-child relationships established during childhood have an enduring quality. Children's experiences of being nurtured by caregivers create strong socio-emotional bonds that continue into adulthood. Children raised continuously by their parents also have a shared history, class and culture (Howe & Feast, 2001, p. 364).

Once making this discovery, Saroo phoned his adoptive parents noting that the reunion with his biological family didn't "change who you are. I love you mom, so much, and you dad," illustrating the understanding that the past does not minimize the love nor does it "devalues the positive adoption experience nor affects the strength of the adopted person's ties with their adoptive family" (Howe & Feast, 2001, p. 363-364). In fact, research suggest that "contact had helped them (adoptees) to realise that the birth mother posed no risk to them or threat to their parental role" (MacDonald & McSherry, 2011, p. 11) and person [is] more likely to remain in contact with their adoptive mother than their birth mother, the frequency of contact with the adoptive mother is likely to be greater than that for the birth mother" (Howe & Feast, 2001, p. 363).

Saroo's success in locating his birth location and birth family provided an opportunity for him to have all of his "questions answered. There are no more dead ends" as he stated. In his process, parts of his identity were revealed; even his correct name: Sheru. The curiosity, search and reunion he experienced fostered his ability to fully integrate his past and present. In doing so, his journey led him to introduce his adoptive mother to his home of origin in India where both mothers met. Footage captured both mothers greet one another tearfully in joyful embrace around Saroo's life and findings. As a result of all of his efforts, his steps in fear, anticipation, and dismay; Saroo's biography creates hope in those who search for loves lost.

BEST PSYCHOLOGY IN FILM

## *SUE BRIERLEY*

Performed by: Nicole Kidman

# *AGAPE*

> *"The only way love can last a lifetime is if it's unconditional. The truth is this: love is not determined by the one being loved but rather by the one choosing to love."*
> – Stephen Kendrick, *The Love Dare*

**SUE:** You've come a long way haven't you? Hum? Little one. And I'm sure it hasn't been easy. One day you'll tell me all about it. You'll tell me everything, who you are, everything. I'll always listen. Always.

Sue Brierley, performed by Nicole Kidman, was based upon the true Sue Brierley who along with her husband John, (acted by David Wenham), adopted the young Saroo, (Sunny Pawar), from an orphanage in Calcutta, India. Upon Saroo's arrival, the Brierley family immediately exhibited unconditional positive regard towards him. Once welcoming Saroo within their home in Australia, Sue alerted him that she would always be a resource in his life. Soon thereafter, the Brierley's adopted a second son with special needs. "Parental love is the love most commonly thought genuinely unconditional" (Cordner, 2016, p. 2). Current theories suggest that unconditional love is similar to the love that is "often labeled with the Greek word agape" (Cordner, 2016, p. 2) defined as "unselfish love of one person for another without sexual implications; brotherly love, Christian love" (Dictionary.com, 2018). The concept of agape and unconditional love is presently considered perhaps an aspirational ideal. If Sue Brierley's love for her sons within the film *Lion* was not one of unconditional love due to the inability of such a love to exist between humans, how can we understand the presence of the all accepting, powerful love between this parent and children?

"Throughout history, scholars across an array of disciplines have speculated on the nature of love" (Regan, 2016, p. 28). Within our current time, "unconditional love gets mentioned quite often these days. The commonest context, and the most often thought to offer the best grip on the idea, is the love of parents for their children" (Cordner, 2016, p. 2). James' works originally published in 1890 described the presence of a "maternal love" where the "essential elements are intense devotion and selflessness" (Regan, 2016, p. 28). Theorists such as Fromm (1956) suggested that because of the nature of the love between parent and child, it "is distinguished from other varieties by its unconditional and altruistic nature" (Regan, 2016, p. 28). Unconditional love suggests that one will love the person for whom they are, under all circumstances as "unconditional love, surely, cannot fail, just because one who loves unconditionally loves, and would love, come what may" (Cordner, 2016, p. 2). Consequent to the above standards, "most people find it hard to practice unconditional love" (Blatt, Ogaki & Yaguchi, 2015, p. 226). Individuals are inclined to question whether unconditional love is a concept that can be placed successfully into practice. Rather, caring relationships that include the presence of unconditional actions tend to be described as unconditional positive regard; a concept introduced by humanistic psychologist Carl Rogers who developed client-centered therapy. Unconditional positive regard suggests that one will value "the person as doing their best to move forward in their lives constructively and respecting the person's right to self-determination no matter what they choose to do" (Joseph, 2012).

Sue dedicated her energies to provide positive regard to both of her children. It was important to her that her children were welcomed into a loving home. Sue was patient in learning about her sons. She was particular curious regarding Saroo's journey; his past experiences of becoming lost in Calcutta, a city that was days' distance from his family of origin. When Saroo became older, she learned that his family experienced poverty. She listened to him recall his childhood memories fondly due to the love and nurturance he received from his biological family. Additionally, when the Brierley's adopted their second adopted son, within moments, Sue became aware that he would require interventions to assist with his global functioning; specifically modulating his affect. Once the children became adults, Sue described her second son, that many would experience as challenging, as a

> tricky little thing. Pure energy. Very incredible. He's been hard to control, but very, very smart. Very…I mean he could do anything if he could learn to control that energy; he could do it, he could do it all.

Adopting became a vehicle for Sue to bestow the love that she had upon children in need while providing unconditional love and regard to them throughout their lives. She further stated,

> we both felt that the world has enough people in it. To have a child, there's no guarantee that we would make anything better. But to take a child that's suffering, like you boys were. Give you a chance in the world. That's something.

**What Makes This Character Rich?**

And Sue provided her boys something. Her love transcended the pain that she experienced when she felt distant in her relationship with both of her children once they became adults. Her love continued despite the importance she placed on being aware of her son Saroo's dreams and pursuits and feeling unaware that he desired to pursue his family of origin. While others may feel threatened given a child's desire to locate their biological family and "feel left out when the adoptee is in Reunion" with their birth family (Lifton, B.J., 2010, p. 75); Sue's response to Saroo was, "I really hope she's there. She needs to see how beautiful you are." Sue understood the benefits of keeping "the communication lines open with their child so that he does not have to retreat" (Lifton, B.J., 2010, p. 78) to maintain connection to her children. Sue also created a supportive environment that fostered remaining knowledgeable of her children's needs and desires. Willing to share her gracious experience of having the opportunity to raise Saroo with his family of origin in the absence of fear, jealousy, or hurt made her a beacon to the belief that "it is not enough to take them out of harm's way," (Schimmel, 2008, p. 217). Rather,

> it is particularly urgent that caregivers empower them to orient their lives in a positive direction by demonstrating to them in the most tangible way that their lives matter, that they are significant individuals, bearers of and deserving of dignity, love and respect (Schimmel, 2008, p. 219).

Cordner's (2016) theory that there is an absence of true unconditional love between individuals where he suggests, "perhaps the concept or idea of unconditional love is best thought of as a kind of ideal, in the light of which we can measure or judge our own loving and find it to be wanting" (p. 3) is challenging within this film. Sue's love that she exhibited to her sons surpassed the denotation of unconditional positive regard and supported the criteria of unconditional love: agape. Sue's love for her two children was unquestionable where she loved them, despite "come what may."

Sue's desires for her children and motivation to care for them became abundantly present when she stated,

**SUE:** "I could have had children."

**SAROO:** "What?"

**SUE:** "We chose not to have kids. We wanted the two of you. That's what we wanted. We wanted the two of you in our lives, that's what we chose."

"Well, of course, 'all parents'—alright, not all but most!— love their children" (Cordner, 2016, p. 6). Sue Brierley was demonstrative of the love she held for her children and was willing to support them through positive times in life and moments that caused them great pain and sorrow. Despite the transitions that her children encountered within their development, Sue remained dedicated to loving her sons in a manner where her needs and desires for affirmation and love were placed in a position that was secondary to their needs without contest. For Sue, adopting children placed her in a position of gratitude, "I've been blessed, very blessed," she relished. "So, loving unconditionally—as implying loving 'come what may'—involved continuing to love despite whatever does or might happen to one's beloved" (Cordner, 2016, p. 2) was offered within this film. Sue was depicted as one who "loved fully, and would continue to love" her "son(s) all the days of their lives" (Getter, 2012, p. 1040).

BEST PSYCHOLOGY IN FILM

## *MANCHESTER BY THE SEA*
Directed by: Kenneth Lonergan

## *SCENE I*

*A view of the lake and its surrounds are presented. Claudia Marie (the Chandler's fishing boat) travels upon the water. Lee and Young Patrick stand talking while Patrick's father, Lee's brother drives the boat.*

**LEE:** (fades in) "….a lot of stuff that he doesn't understand about the world that I understand that, that makes—That makes all my actions when I move through the world-- I do things better, 'cause I can see it all laid out like looking at a map. Have you ever looked at a map?

**PATRICK:** "Yes!"

**LEE:** "Do you know how to read a map?"

**PATRICK:** "But, I'm not mistaken."

**LEE:** "Do you know how to read a map?"

**PATRICK:** "Yeah."

**LEE:** "Your father's a perfectly good guy, but it is a lot of stuff that he just doesn't understand about the world that I understand."

**PATRICK:** "My dad is better!"

**LEE:** "Wait, wait listen."

**PATRICK:** "My dad is better!"

**LEE:** "Hun, I have, I haven't asked you a question yet. I haven't asked you a question.

*Young Patrick runs towards the front of the boat towards his father playfully.*

**PATRICK:** "My dad is better!"

*Young Patrick runs around making loud noise. Lee leans in and grabs him from the back embracing him.*

**LEE:** "Listen to me, listen, don't tell you father. Shut up! Be quiet. Shush. Be quiet. I haven't asked you a question yet. I haven't asked you anything. Listen. Shh. Quiet. We got it. Don't worry. Listen. If there was-- if you could take one guy to a island with you and you knew you'd be safe cause he was the best man, and he was gonna to figure out how to survive, he was gonna make everything, gonna make the world a good place on the island, he was gonna keep you happy, he--this is the best man for the job, no matter what; if it were between me and your father, who would you take?"

**PATRICK:** "My daddy."

**LEE:** "I don't see. Hang on a second."

*Young Patrick begins toward the front of the boat continuing the banter.*

**LEE:** "Hang on a second, hang on a second. Listen, I think you're wrong about that. It's your choice to make, but I want you to understand something. That there's a lot of…"

*Young Patrick arrives to the front of the boat and holds a fish.*

**LEE:** "Hey! Pick up—What hap-- what is that? You can't leave your fishing rod like that."

# *GRIEF*

> *"Death is not the greatest loss in life. The greatest loss is what dies inside us while we live."*
>
> – Norman Cousin

When disasters happen, life changes. Whether the event is a natural disaster such as a hurricane, tornado, earthquake, flood or a disaster caused by human action, such as negligence, error or the like (Xu, 2012), life is altered, and things cannot go back to the way they once were. The death of a child is a significant life stressor and is emotionally upsetting for a family (Vega, Soledad Rivera & Gonzalez, 2014). In particular, the death of a child "leads to more intense and persistent grief and depression than the loss of a sibling, spouse, [and] parent" (Neria & Litz, 2003), according to researchers. Within the film, *Manchester by the Sea*, directed by Kenneth Lonergan, the protagonist Lee Chandler, performed by Casey Affleck, is an individual stricken by grief due to the death of his children and the loss of his marriage. "It is terribly difficult, for example, after losing a child, to realize: 'My child is dead and will never come back,' especially if the loss occurred under traumatic circumstances and this thought is accompanied by unpleasant images" (Boelen, 2016, p. 6). Exposure to disasters, whether natural or human made, creates a period after the loss, which is termed bereavement.

Bereavement, defined as "1. a period of mourning after a loss, especially after the death of a loved one; 2. a state of intense grief, as after the loss of a loved one; desolation" (Merriam Webster Dictionary, 2017) suggests that an individual after the death of children experiences a period of anticipated "acute grief…a state of acute emotional distress" (Boelen, 2016, p. 2). According to

Bowlby (1980), bereavement was understood to be a psychological stressor due to the absence loss creates. As a result, when one has lost a close attachment bond that created positive feelings of security and safety, a time of bereavement begins. Once loss occurs, bereavement continues, though grief, (the feelings that accompany the loss), transforms with time. "Grief is a syndrome of cognitions, emotions and behaviors that often arise together following the death of a loved one" (Robinaugh, LeBland, Vuletich & McNally, 2014, p. 510). Grief also includes reactions that are physical, spiritual, and social (Smit, 2015). There is no one specific manner or a correct way to navigate grief (Simon, 2013). However, many individuals follow a conventional grieving process; where over time, feelings of grief subsides, and one is able to cohere the loss of the individual and the meaning of death in a manner where typical social, occupational, and personal functioning resume. This process is referred to as "integrated grief", where feelings of grief remain, the deceased is not forgotten, yet the feelings of grief are no longer the central aspect of the person's life (Simon, 2017). Typically, most persons "ultimately adapt to the loss with a reduction in grief intensity and return to a revised but meaningful and satisfying life without the deceased" (Simon, 2013, p. 416) and without intervention assistance.

Distinctly, there are individuals who may be particularly vulnerable to experience persistent grief: ones who have lost a child or partner, during a traumatic event, individuals who experience "collateral misery after the loss," and who are vulnerable prior to the loss (Boelen, 2016, p. 5). The factors that influence a person's risk to prolonged periods of grief "may vary across individuals" (Robinaugh, et al. 2014, p. 512). Boelen (2016) cited research conducted by Keyes et al. (2014) that revealed an unexpected and sudden loss is often followed by the experience of substantial mental health concerns. In particular, parents whose children have died within a disaster are at an increased risk for developing mental health challenges. (Xu, 2012). Further, researchers such as Davis, et al. (1998) and Lichtenthal, et al. (2010) offered data that supports that difficulty in finding meaning in the loss can result in complicated grief and significant levels of distress. Other risk factors include individuals with interpersonal dependency, that when symptoms occur, social separation may materialize which further impacts functioning. Additionally, individuals with a high degree of spousal dependency are equally at high risk "because of the increased risk for preoccupying thoughts related to the deceased and a sense that one's identity, meaning in life, and plans for the future are lost without the deceased" (Robinaugh, et al, 2014, p. 519). Partners find that typical spousal relations may curtail. Lastly, there may be intrapersonal risks. One who believes that the world is unjust, empty, and meaningless after the loss of a loved one is more likely vulnerable to symptoms of persistent grief (Robinaugh, et al, 2014). However, specific risk factors that cause one to experience various health challenges coupled with knowledge of how these variables interact to heighten or lower risks remain unknown (Stroebe, et al., 2017).

Additional consequences that occur after the loss of a loved one may involve the experience of mental health issues (Xi, 2012). Specifically, individuals may become fixed in grief when one losses a child/children. Boelen (2016) noted that Wijngaards-De Meij et al. shared the concept that children distinguishes one's identity, one's perception of self, and defines time: the past, present, and future. The manner in which the child/children perished and the events that occurred thereafter all influence the progression of one's experienced grief (Boelen, 2016).

During the beginning of the film, Lee is presented with the tragedy of his two daughters and son caught in the family home that is engulfed flames. Lee sees firefighters recover the remains of his children, carried in black bags as he communicates to police officers. Though his wife is rescued from the fire, years after the couple is found divorced and Lee lives an independent life. He is reintroduced as one who holds multiple vulnerabilities to experience persistent grief and demonstrates a presentation of one crippled by sorrow.

Loss is a common, inherent part of life. A response to one's quietus such as grieving "is a normal reaction to loss" (Boss & Carnes, 2012, p. 462). One progresses through a natural emotional experience in an effort to process the deaths. With time "gradually, around the sadness and pain, one gets more room for new activities and new relationships" (Boelen, 2016, p. 2). "It is a serious mistake to confuse normal forms of suffering with psychopathology, particularly the suffering resulting from traumatic loss" (Thieleman & Cacciatrore, 2014, p. 120). Grief nor is the time of bereavement considered mental health concerns (Boss & Carnes, 2012). In contrast, research supports recent views that grief and bereavement are occurrences to be worked through where resuming a positive disposition with rapidity is not necessary or expected (McNeish, 2013). Bereft parents' "grief responses may indeed appear abnormal" (Thieleman & Cacciatrore, 2014, p. 117). Neria and Litz (2003) posited that reactions to loss are "universal and tremendously variable" (p. 74) and despite the circumstances around the death, grief is anticipated to be a temporary emotional state.

Awareness has heightened that "the experience of the death of a loved one is a major and central experience in life, which has been associated with different trajectories and outcomes" (Fernandez-Alcantara, Perez-Garcia, Perez-

Marfil, Catena-Martinez, Hueso-Montoro, Cruz-Quintana, 2016, p. 260). Specifically, "a combination of their (grief and bereavement) high intensity and long duration is abnormal reconciles the belief that all grief symptoms are normal, but not all grieving processes are normal" (Maciejewski, Maercker, Bolen & Prigerson, 2016, p. 272). "In general, most bereaved people eventually adapt well, although many suffer severely in the early weeks and months of bereavement" (Stroebe, et al., 2017, p. 348). For some, amongst the bereft, there is a small percent of individuals, approximately ten to fifteen percent, (Fernandez-Alcantara, et al., 2016) "who fail to return to normal functioning; they are stuck with a degree of steady mourning and functional impairment" (Neria & Litz, 2003, p. 74). Challenges with progression through bereavement may be attributed to difficulties with coping with the loss. Coping is a process that activates the use of various strategies to assist with managing challenging situations that fosters tolerance and reduces stressors caused by bereavement (Stroebe & Schut, 2010). When symptoms of grief become an impairment to one's overall functioning for a substantial amount of time, one may exhibit symptoms of mental heath concerns.

The processes involved with bereavement and grief symptoms have been researched throughout the years. In fact, Freud introduced the study of grief where he hypothesized that "mourning is a reaction of adapting oneself in a relatively passive and universal process, whose main objective is the elaboration of detachment toward the dead person" (Vega, et al., 2014, p. 167). Since, concepts of grieving have evolved. Over the last fifty years, great progress has been made in the diversity of thought regarding what actions materialize during bereavement.

In the late 1960s, grief began to be conceptualized as an operation that transpire with the completion of linear stages (Kubler-Ross, 1969) with the thought that if completed correctly, the mourning process would come to a proper conclusion (Boss & Carnes, 2012). "The obvious appeal of stages is that they order chaos and lend predictability to the uncertainty of grieving" (Anderson, 2010, p. 133). Studies suggest that grief occurs with progressions and regressions and do not always follow a predictable path. "Grief is a distinct individual, social, and relational experience" (Neria & Litz, 2003, p. 73) and "the danger with thinking about stages is that the uniqueness of each grief is overlooked and the unpredictable circularity of grieving is subsumed under a 'one-size-fits all' linear process" (Anderson, 2010, p. 133). McNeish (2003) further concurred that, "what is clear is that simplistic models of grief fail to capture the complexity of grieving" (p. 194) and "perhaps the most important lesson of the last twenty years' research and theorizing is the danger of simplistic application of any model to real life bereavement" (p. 195).

We have now come to understand that grief models may be "most useful when considered as a framework upon which grieving can be negotiated rather than as a mould into which grieving must fit" (McNeish, 2013). In the 1980s, Worden reported upon the concept of the Task Model, which suggested that those in mourning do not move through stages but perform a number of tasks over time (Vega, et al, 2014; Smit, 2015), which may not occur in a linear fashion.

> Worden's four-phase model involves engagement with four tasks: to accept the reality of the loss, work through the pain of grief, adapt to a new environment and find enduring connection with the deceased while learning to live without them (Smit, 2015, p. 35).

Additionally, in 1995 Stroebe and Schut created the dual-process model of grief. This theory offered that individuals vacillate between "two categories of stressors associated with bereavement, namely those that are loss-versus-restoration oriented" (Stroebe & Schut, 2010, p. 277). This model noted that the oscillations between these two stressors allow one time to grieve by expressing and controlling one's feelings. For instance, loss-orientation fosters the focus on grief work and assessing aspects of loss where restoration-orientation may include conceptualizing how one has changed since the loss and how one will navigate the world thereafter (Stroebe & Schut, 2010).

Further, the meaning making model inspired by the book Man's Search for Meaning by Victor Frankl's experience describing his discovery of meaning during his incarceration in a Nazi concentration camp was reconstructed by Neimeyer and colleagues in 2011. This model was framed to be applicable when working with individuals suffering from an illness. It indicated that finding meaning in the loss fosters positive outcomes where challenges with finding meaning to the loss is more likely to lead to negative adaptation (Smit, 2015).

Within current psychological literature, there is also "growing recognition among scholars and clinicians that, after the death of a loved one, a significant minority of people develop persistent and debilitating symptoms of grief" (Boelen & Prigerson, p. 771). In response to this awareness, "during the last decade, a great deal of research has been conducted between adaptive and non-adaptive patterns of grief and the specific emotional dysregulations" that occur as a result of prolonged grief symptoms (Fernandez-Alcantara, et al., 2016, p. 260). Researchers have frequently utilized the names prolonged grief disorder (PGD), complicated grief and, most recently, persistent complex bereavement disorder (PCBD) to articulate behaviors observed during prolonged bereavement. Findings from such research provides conclusive corroboration "demonstrating that prolonged grief disorder (PGD)-intense, prolonged symptoms of grief, coupled with some form of functional impairment beyond 6 months post-loss—constitutes a distinct mental disorder" (Maciejewski, et al., 2016, p. 266). The *Diagnostic and Statistical Manual ($5^{th}$ ed.)*, (DSM-5) has offered the use of a unitary diagnostic criteria coined persistent complex bereavement disorder (PCBD) to capture such symptomatology.

At present, PCBD is a condition within the DSM-5 located in a section that recommends diagnostic criteria for further study. Within the DSM-5, PCBD opens with information that alerts "the specific items, thresholds, and durations contained in these research criteria sets were set by expert consensus" (American Psychiatric Association). Though PCBD is not a formal diagnostic disorder within the DSM-5, this suggested disorder and its criteria exist to provide clinicians a common language to utilize to facilitate discussions and research of the proposed symptom set.

Because there are three frequently utilized terminologies to describe similar phenomenon of grief during times of bereavement, which is the most appropriate to utilize at this time? Maciejewski, et al. (2016) performed a study to determine whether the terms prolonged grief disorder (PGD), complicated grief and PCBD were similar in identifying diagnostic criteria. The authors' data revealed that prolonged grief disorder and PCBD resulted in no significant differences. Data yielded that "PGD and PCBD identify the same diagnostic entity. Therefore, the difference between PGD and PCBD is mainly semantic" (Maciejewski, et al., 2016, p. 271). However, results noted that complicated grief criteria held "moderate agreement" with prolonged grief disorder and PCBD. Due to the context of examining psychological dynamics within cinema, the consistency PCBD holds with prolonged grief disorder and the prior and continued use of the DSM-5 to illustrate diagnostic criteria found within these subjects, the remaining and subsequent chapters discussing *Manchester by the Sea* will utilize the diagnostic term PCBD for continuity.

PCBD is characterized by symptoms that arise when one has experienced a death with whom he/she had a close relationship. Since the death, the individual experiences at least one of the following behaviors more days than not to a clinically significant degree: persistent yearning/longing for the deceased, intense sorrow, and emotional pain in response to the death, preoccupation with the deceased and/or preoccupation with the circumstances of the death. For these individuals, one or more of these symptoms must be present for more than twelve months with adults. In addition, the individual will have reactive distress to the death. Specific symptoms may include having marked difficulty in accepting the death, experiencing disbelief or emotional numbness over the loss, having difficulty engaging in positive reminiscing about the deceased, bitterness or anger related to the loss, possessing maladaptive appraisals about oneself in relation to the deceased or the death that can take the form of self-blame, and engaging in excessive avoidance of reminders of the loss. Lastly, an individual experiencing symptoms of PCBD will also experience identity and social disruption that can include a desire to die in an effort to be with the deceased, having difficulty trusting individuals after the death, feeling alone or detached from others, lacking a sense of meaning in life, feeling empty in the absence of the deceased, experiencing confusion about one's purpose and role in life where a diminished sense of one's own identity occurs, having difficulty or reluctance to pursue in interests since the loss or fails to plan for the future in relation to friendships and activities. The bereaved may not experience all of the mentioned criteria, however, must exhibit six or more of the above symptoms of reactive distress to the death in combination to social/identity disruption that significantly negatively impacts the person's daily functioning. Further, for this condition to be present, symptoms must be out of proportion and inconsistent with what is expected from the person's cultural and religious practices.

The manner in which one copes with loss is varying and is influenced by a number of variables. "Several factors, including the nature of the attachment, how the person died, and their past history, religious beliefs, personality, age, gender and ethnicity" (Smit, 2015, p. 33) affect the ways in which grief is experienced. "Another consideration is that different cultures vary in the ways that they experience and express grief and loss" (Smit, 2015, p. 33). In the United States, the culture of grieving encourages an individual to successfully conclude bereavement within a specific time frame. At that time, the bereaved is described as being able to reach a sense of emotional closure. Research suggests that individuals yearn for closure to occur. However, "the continuous use of *closure* among various professionals perpetuate the myth that grief has a demarcated end, and that it is emotionally healthier to close the door on grief than to live with it" (Boss & Carnes, 2012, p. 459).

Lee's character is depicted as an individual whose presentation is inhibited from progressing in a manner that allows for his grief to feel manageable on a day-to-day basis. He experienced intense emotional pain after the death of his children. He had difficulty engaging in positive reminiscing about his past, possessed a maladaptive appraisal of himself, isolated from others, avoided reminders of the town in which he lost his family, struggled to understand his role in life and was reluctant to plan for the future. His grieving produced clinically significant symptoms that remained present over the course of years and negatively impacted his global functioning. As such, Lee's emotional presentation was one that matched and warranted consideration of the pending diagnosis of PCBD.

Lee was most impacted by social and identity disruption: the lack of motivation to connect to others and struggle to plan accordingly for his nephew's (Patrick) future once awarded guardianship of him. Most notable was Lee's overall personality or identity differences. In earlier scenes, Lee was shown as an engaged, working family man who initiated positive exchanges with his family. After the death of his children, Lee became a shell of the man he once was. The death of his children and loss of his marriage seemed to take his life and leave a corpse in its wake.

Our knowledge and understanding of grief and bereavement has advanced significantly regarding how one grieves during bereavement. "Research over the past two decades has shown that the grief experience is complex, and recent conceptualisations have emphasised that grief is a personal journey that is never the same for any two people" (Smit, 2015, p. 33). Individuals who continue to grieve can be isolated from others and thought to be pathological (Boss and Carnes, 2012). The bereft can exhibit symptoms that make it challenging to connect with them due to the difficulty they experience navigating their pain. "Grief ultimately teaches us all the same lesson: to value the relationship, experiences and time that we have in this present moment" (Smit, 2015, p. 36).

BEST PSYCHOLOGY IN FILM

## *LEE CHANDLER*

Performed by: Casey Affleck

# *BEREAVEMENT*

> *"Relationships take up energy; letting go of them, psychiatrists theorize, entails mental work. When you lose someone you were close to, you have to reassess your picture of the world and your place in it. The more your identity was wrapped up with the deceased, the more difficult the loss."*
>
> – Meghan O'Rourke (2010)

"Losing a child is recognized as especially disruptive and challenging to the expected order of life events: The young ought to outlive the old" (Bogensperger & Lueger-Schuster, 2014, p. 1). When one's child, and in the event of Lee Chandler, one's children perish, grieving and finding meaning in the losses can feel insurmountable. Lee Chandler, within the film, *Manchester by the Sea*, is an individual who presents with debilitating feelings of grief surrounding the death of his children. As a result, Lee's overall functioning becomes compromised which caused him to struggle to navigate, years later, the death of his brother and accept the responsibility to being his nephew's, Patrick, legal guardian.

At the onset of the film, Lee was introduced as a man and father who expressed a typical range of emotion. For example, within the opening scene, Lee was observed enjoying time with his brother and nephew upon their boat. He actively engaged with his family, spoke frequently with reciprocal exchanges, and evoked positive feelings in his nephew. He made jokes and was presented as lighthearted.

Lee was also seen as possessing a loving relationship with his wife and children. When he entered the room, he initiated interactions with his daughters, ensured that they exchanged loving affections, was the impetus to positive, playful exchanges with his wife, and provided affection to his son. Globally, Lee was portrayed as an emotionally expressive man who readily partook in social relations. Additionally, he had fun times that were accompanied by laughter and camaraderie. Lee's socializations, affective expression and life were globally conventional in nature.

After the death of his children, Lee's functioning significantly declined and became impaired. During the investigation with officials, Lee recalled the events leading to the fire that took the lives of his children. His emotional presentation immediately thereafter was drastically and forever changed. Lee's ability to cope with the trauma was limited. He attempted to escape his reality by drawing the gun of a police officer to attempt suicide. Subsequently, he was depicted as a man whose life and overall emotional functioning was halted and remained diminished for the foreseeable duration of the film.

Lee's presentation was similar to criteria found offered within the diagnosis of persistent complex bereavement disorder (PCBD). As noted previously in the Manchester by the Sea section, Lee's experience of intense emotional pain following the death of his children, avoidance of the town in which he was raised (Manchester), difficulty planning for his future, challenges with initiating relationships with others, demonstration of social withdrawal and lack of a solid sense of identity portrayed substantial symptoms that negatively impacted his social and occupational functioning. His symptoms were persistent; lasting years after the tragedy.

Lee was most recognized by others within the community of Manchester for his avoidance of the town. It was noted that Lee visited solely due to his brother's hospitalizations related to symptoms of congestive heart failure. Due to his brother's illness, Lee was required to care for his nephew at times. When he was granted guardianship of Patrick, after his brother's death, Lee was required to relocate his life to Manchester. In doing so, he would face interacting with individuals of his past. Further, because Lee parented his teenaged nephew, he was also requested to begin generating new relationships with members of the community such as the parents of Patrick's friends. As demands increased, Lee's symptoms became heighten and significantly pronounced. Consequently, the influence of his symptoms of PCBD grew increasingly apparent to all around him.

Affectively, Lee's emotions were restricted. His approach to affective expression appeared to be a direct consequence of the trauma in which he experienced. "The loss of a child leaves an enormous gap in parents, creating loneliness, frustration, and guilt" (Vega, et al., 2014, p. 169). Lee was less likely to articulate his emotions; and, as a result, due to his limited range of expressed emotions, it made it difficult for individuals to gauge how he was feeling within given situations. Specifically, Lee tended to maneuver through his life after the death of his children and the loss of his marriage with blunted affect. He appeared distant from others and reframed from expressing a typical range of emotion such as happiness, sadness, and disappointment to name a few. His presentation caused him to appear to others as "rude and unfriendly; I get these complaints all the time," his boss stated regarding how others perceived him. For example, Lee was observed performing janitorial work duties. His clients shared information and he frequently overheard comments that may have been considered emotionally provocative to most. Despite what was conveyed, Lee's emotional response remained steady and unaffected by others. Whether one professed sexual fantasies about him or a person shared their experience of the loss of a loved one, Lee presented with a consistent flat affect giving no rise or concern to the situation. Presenting as such allowed Lee to both approach and respond to each situation in a similar fashion, calmly in an effort to accomplish his tasks in the absence of becoming emotionally involved.

In situations that elicited strong emotion, Lee utilized a problem-focused coping approach to manage situations. "Problem–focused coping is directed at managing and changing the problem causing the distress" (Stroebe & Schut, 2010, p. 277). When Lee approached his brother's physician, nurse, and a family friend, (George, performed by C.J. Wilson), regarding the death of his brother, Lee asked clarifying, direct questions to gain the details regarding what occurred. Exhibition of his upset was expressed by the use of one word, a profanity. After a moment of silence from all, Lee apologized and resumed asking questions and gaining information that allowed him to determine what actions needed to occur after leaving the hospital. Though the nurse attempted to touch him to provide comfort, Lee was non-responsive to the empathy offered. Due to his lack of acceptance of the gesture, the nurse returned her arm to her side, appearing uncertain as to how to provide comfort to him.

Once learning of the nature of his brother's death, Lee was soon informed that his brother constructed a will that granted him custody of his nephew, Patrick. During this time, Lee initially exhibited an emotional response of panic; as he was cognizant of his limitations and understood that he was unfit to care for him. Lee's sense of normality discontinued after the death of his children; where, thereafter, he experienced "paralysis, helplessness and confusion" (Laub & Lee, 2002, p. 435). He expressed disbelief regarding his brother's decision to place him in the role of a guardian to Patrick's upbringing. In turn, Lee was unable to conceive of caring for another. His acute difficulty managing this idea resulted in him responding impulsively in desperation. He questioned whether anyone could and was willing to perform the parenting responsibility. "Do you want to be his guardian?" he asked twice of George. After awkward moments and a negative response, Patrick confronted Lee about his behavior asking, "Are you brain damaged? You just can't talk to people like that!" Lee answered, "I know, it's just the logistics. I just have to work it all out, I swear."

Collecting himself, Lee attempted to resume the use of a problem-focused approach, by grasping at logic and engaging in developing a plan for coordinating details. Rather than respond using an emotion-focused style of coping, as defined by "managing the emotion that results from stress" (Stroebe & Schut, 2010, p. 277), Lee attempted to simplify and incorporate information to create a proposal that could be executed to have Patrick cared for. Creating an alternative to care would free Lee from Manchester and permit resuming his life in Boston. This approach served Lee well in being able to conceptualize what would be required of him. However, the use of logic reinforced his tendency to engage with others using a restricted range of affect during emotionally laden situations. Research indicates that individuals with many symptoms of grief have a lower ability to use emotional decision-making skills (Fernande-Alcantara, et al, 2016). There is also a great deal of support that suggests that these individuals also struggle to regulate their emotions and express affect (Fernande-Alcantara, et al, 2016). Yet, long-term reliance upon logic to problem solve during times that require emotional focus is less effective in healing (Neria & Litz, 2003). In part, Lee's desire to isolate his affect and rely upon logic solely in situations that were affectively loaded hindered his use of specific aspects of executive functioning skills.

Executive functioning is "a central aspect of neuropsychological performance" (Fernandez-Alcantara, 2016, p. 260) and is "a multi-faceted neuro-psychological construct consisting of a set of higher-order neuro-cognitive processes that allow cognitively able organisms to make choices and to engage in purposeful, goal directed, and future-oriented behavior" (Suchy, 2009, p. 106). Individuals with significant symptoms of grief are likely to have difficulty problem solving and when they approach tasks or situations, they are less inclined to use effective methods to achieve a positive outcome (Fernandez-Alcantara, 2016). For Lee these findings are compelling, as his primary mode of managing situations included a problem-solving approach, a method that would be less likely to adequately support him during challenging times. Further, Lee's difficulty in activating his executive functioning skills effectively was experienced as intolerable.

Interpersonally, Lee's use of logic to problem solve during the recent death of his brother did not foster an environment of collaboration and a feeling of togetherness. When at the hospital hearing regarding his brother's death from the doctor, Lee remained factual, though the physician and nurse attempt to comfort him emotionally. When his friend offered to assist him in performing activities that were essential, Lee provided brief unelaborated responses of "thank you" and "thank you very much". The manner in which he responded suggested each task was conceptualized as a responsibility checked off of a list, rather than accept an offer to alleviate stress from a loved one. Though his behavior was expected from one in time of bereavement, Lee's approach to social interactions remained as such for years after the death of his children and endured after his brother died. Lee's global interactions with others was marred by significant deficits in the execution of interpersonal skills and the ability to communicate in an elaborative manner his thoughts and feelings. Fernandez-Alcantara, et al. (2016) shared that fellow researchers have found that individuals "experiencing intense grief had lower scores in verbal fluency, attention, working memory, and semantic memory" (p. 260), which are all critical competencies demonstrated in social exchanges with others.

Lee's ability to generate novel relationships was also an area that was directly affected by his functioning. Though aware of a woman's affections towards him, he struggled to create a positive exchange that included general conversation. In particular, when Lee was invited in the home of Patrick's girlfriend by her mother, Jill (performed by Heather Burns), for dinner, he declined and offered to wait in his vehicle until his nephew completed his visit.

When specifically informed by Patrick of Jill's amiable feelings towards him, he had difficulty creating a connection as illustrated by his inability to develop a casual dialogue despite her various prompts. Hence, Jill responded desperately to her daughter and Patrick that they hurry their homework duties due to Lee's social impairment. Lee's difficulty relating to others was indubitably captured by Jill. She pled, "I can't sit down there much longer. He won't talk. I've been trying to make conversation for a half an hour. I realize that I'm not the most fascinating person in the world, but it is very strained!" Once confronted by Patrick regarding his behaviors, he asked, "You can't make small talk like everyone else?" Lee responded authentically by stating, "Nope."

When presented with conversations that required Lee to be emotionally present and engaged, he frequently noted, "I don't want to talk about this. I can't talk about this right now." Though he suggested he would engage in such conversation at a later time, Lee used the above statements to successfully avoid returning to the discussion unless within the contained structure of a suggestion of action. Patrick questioned regarding how Lee believed his care would look in the future. Patrick desired additional details, such as where he would live and with whom. Lee postponed many of these conversations in the moment to reduce affective interference until he gathered serviceable information to properly discuss the facts rather than become acquainted and share regarding his emotional experience.

Defensively, Lee used many psychological constructs within this film to protect himself from experiencing emotional tensions. His global emotional functioning was regressed, where he navigated his life in a manner that was less advanced than his previous functioning in an effort to avoid the pain associated with his losses. Though regression is a defense mechanism that protects one from emotionally experiencing the negative feelings that result from managing conflicts; his regression as seen in beginning scenes suggest that Lee may have once relied upon advanced defense mechanisms prior to the trauma he experienced. Lee's repertoire of defenses may have been broad, and could have included both primitive and higher-level mechanisms. However, within the film that illustrated the life of Lee Chandler primarily after the death of his children and the loss of his marriage, his character firmly utilized the above noted defense of regression as well as isolation of affect, avoidance, acting out, and withdrawal.

Isolation of affect as described as "separating an idea from its associated affect state to avoid emotional turmoil" (Gabbard, 2005, p. 36) is a defense mechanism that Lee evinced frequently. Many times, during emotionally charged situations, his approach of gaining information to best resolve the problem in the absence of expressing emotion was successful for him. As he was able to successfully complete tasks during stressful times, experiencing the affect that was elicited within the situations was viewed as a distraction or hindrance to accomplish the demand. Thus, engaging with emotionally challenging situations became increasingly tolerable for Lee with the use of isolation of affect.

Lee actively avoided emotion in which he felt ill equipped to manage. When posed with tense situations, he possessed the ability to articulate that he was unable to engage in the conversation. At times, Lee was less likely to use avoidance and allowed his anger and other negative affect to be felt and expressed. During these regressed states, Lee relied upon further primitive defenses to manage his emotions. Specifically, he engaged in physical aggression and activated the defense mechanism of acting out his feelings of pain and aggressive urges. For instance, once intoxicated, his negative emotions were less restrained by the structure of logic and problem solving. Under the influence of alcohol, Lee did not verbalize his feelings, yet became aggressive with others; punching and initiating physical altercations with no apparent provocation. Lee's acting out behaviors where he welcomed aggressive interactions with others placed him in numerous unsafe situations. Many times, his behaviors caused him to become physically hurt within these brawls. Those who cared for him ensured that his belligerent behavior discontinued, indicative of a pattern of such behavioral demonstrations.

Further, Lee primarily utilized the use of withdrawal; a predominate defense mechanism that was most observant with others in his life. Individuals choose to withdraw from social activities for various reasons that may include the belief that since the trauma "the world has become a dangerous" (Boelen, 2016, p. 8) place where "others withdraw because they think that continuing usual social activities will not provide them with any satisfaction" (Boelen,

2016, p. 8). For Lee, after the death of his children, it appeared that his trauma was ineffable, and situations since felt trivial. Lee's social isolation and withdrawal appeared to originate from the later hypothesis Boelen offers where he no longer yielded pleasure from engaging with others. Lee's pervasive social withdrawal tended to impede his ability to create and maintain relationships that caused his interpersonal relationships to be severely impaired. Though his nephew encouraged him to engage with others, Lee lacked motivation to invest. He presented with a dearth of desire for connections in combination with a deficiency in accessing his sense of self. Due to his lack of understanding of his role in life, it hindered him from being capable of offering others an element of himself that might cultivate a relationship.

As a guardian, Lee also fumbled to grasp the nature of his role. Many times, Patrick grew frustrated with Lee's emotional presentation. Though Patrick was aware that Lee was concerned regarding his wellbeing as illustrated by Lee's desire to secure a future plan for Patrick, Patrick desired more from Lee emotionally than what he was able to provide. Alternatively, Lee furnished Patrick with logistics and many times afforded Patrick the liberty to agree or rebuke his ideas by noting, "This is the way that I planned it. It's up to you."

"The death of a child causes parents such profound pain and suffering that it is very difficult to heal" (Vega, et al., 2014, p. 169). At the conclusion of the film, it remained clear that Lee was unsuccessful in coping effectively from the death of his children and divorce. "I just can't get past this," he stated. "The people whom we loved are always with us in some way" (Boss & Carnes, 2012, p. 459). For Lee, memories of his children, his marriage, and brother were memories of sorrow that lived on. "The work of grieving is an alternation between remembering and hoping. Remembering liberates the past by admitting the finality of death and hoping frees the future to possibility" (Anderson, 2010, p. 135). As Lee recalled his loved ones, he never let them die in mind; and, he refused to carry on and live. It appeared that Lee was acutely aware that "real grief is not healed by time. The only way out of grief is through the pain" (Anderson, 2010, p. 134). At the close of the film, Lee lacked refuge from the pain and strength to go through the grief. Due to the level of compromise his symptoms induced over the quality of his life; he was rendered incapacitated and unable to follow through with his brother's arranged plan to care for Patrick.

"Parents who have been able to survive [the death of a loved one] relate that one of the aspects that helped is learning to accept and bear their pain and suffering for the rest of their lives" (Vega, et al., 2014, p. 169). Lee reported authentically that the grief he experienced was unable to be weathered; the grief would remain with him. "Because we are simultaneously relational and finite creatures, we will inevitably lose people and things to which we are attached. There is no love without loss" (Anderson, 2009, p. 127). Lee's life experience was well acquainted with this phenomenon. "Consistent with newer models of parental grief, parental narratives also emphasized that the grief journey after the loss of a child is never-ending; however, the character and intensity of their grief changed over time" (Snaman, Kaye, Torres, Gibson, Baker, 2016, p. 1596). Changes within Lee's bereavement and his grief symptoms lacked progression despite time, which caused consistent emotional distress.

"Grief is about relationships; about our caring and connecting and loving…[it] is a reminder that death is a part of life" (Smit, 2015, p. 33). Lee's gross challenges with moving through and living with his grief sacrificed his ability to reengage with the world in a meaningful way. "For all loss, grief requires patience" (Boss & Carnes, 2012, p. 466). "If we limit our attachments in order to diminish grief, we risk fleeing from the fullness of life in order to avoid the pain of loss" (Anderson, 2010, p. 127). As Lee signed the paperwork that allowed George to adopt Patrick, we learn that Lee's ability to participate in the world remained modified by the losses he experienced.

**What Makes This Character Rich?**

Lee Chandler is a complex character, one that is multi-dimensional despite his regressed personality style and behaviors. One aspect that makes Lee of interest is the ability to witness his emotional functioning prior to the traumatic deaths and losses. The audience is able to view Lee as a typical working male, married, with children, and friends. His life and experience was conventional in nature. The juxtaposition from his previous functioning to the manner in which he functioned thereafter was described by his ex-wife as: "I see you walking around here, you are dead." One is able to empathize with the severity of Lee's unyielding pain that inhibited him from being able to reengage fully in life. The viewers are able to observe the direct effects of PCBD that arises in a typical family man. We are able to observe through Lee's story that every person can experience a significant change in life. Life as we know it can change in minutes and deficits in global functioning is a shared vulnerability to all.

Lee's character is also generously plenteous in the manner in which it extends a model to consider the death instinct. For those who have contemplated regarding the death instinct that Freud introduced into the works of psychology (1920), this film is an excellent depiction of this phenomenon. Though there are many ways to engage with the death instinct as highlighted in the work of Winnicott, a psychoanalyst who was influential to object relations theory, Klein, a psychoanalyst and innovator within object relation theory, Kohut, a self psychologist and others, according to Freud, the death instinct is a desire to return and restore life to an earlier stage (Freud, 1920). Laub & Lee (2002) shared that within Freud's works this instinct involves the use of masochism, aggression and sadism and can include primitive defense mechanisms (e.g., denial, dissociation, depersonalization, derealization and splitting). Lee's initial desire to take his life within the police station, and, thereafter, his incapacity to initiate drive, generate new relationships (both social and romantic), his expression of anger that posed a threat to his physical integrity and challenges with taking an active role in maintaining previous relationships illustrate masochism and the use of aggression to express his emotions. Specifically, his masochism manifested in the presence of a death that is acknowledged by his ex-wife's concern for his wellbeing. These variables are echoed in his personal acknowledgement of being defeated by grief.

Additionally, the range and quality of defenses mechanisms Lee utilized was impressively illustrated within this film. Lee's regressed emotional presentation facilitates the use of both primitive defense mechanisms that included acting out and withdrawal as well as progressive, higher-level defenses such as displacement and isolation of affect. The positive results of using defenses were observable while an equal opportunity to witness the unfavorable consequences that occur when defenses become primitive was also provided. Lastly, there has been

> a shift away from the notion that successful grieving requires mourners to be able to 'let go and get on with life,' to a move towards accepting that while we are changed by our loss, our relationships with our departed loved one's remains and is transformed (Smit, 2015, p. 33).

Lee's global response to the death of his children and additional losses thereafter evidenced the concept that life is forever changed by grieving loved one deaths. During Lee's prolonged grief, he utilized a number of mechanisms that assisted him with being able to function with less compromise. His practical logical approach enabled him to effectively solve problems. His demonstration of stable and predictable thought processes fostered his problem-solving success. Yet, Lee experienced significant challenges integrating and modulating his affect where he easily became flooded with emotion, responded in shock, and related to others in an unorthodox manner. In relation to his grief, there were times when Lee disabled his use of logic and acted out using impulsive, aggressive behaviors while demonstrating poor judgment and respect for the safety of himself and others. The fluctuation in his thought processes, range of defense mechanisms, accurate portrayal of symptoms related to PCBD and flirtation with the death instinct contributed to the wealth of this character. Accordingly, due to the magnitude of this depiction, Casey Affleck (Lee Chandler) was nomination for an Academy Award® and earned Best Actor in a Leading Role.

BEST PSYCHOLOGY IN FILM

## PATRICK CHANDLER

Performed by: Lucas Hedges

# COPING

> *"One can only imagine the depth of the loss and the developmental confusion that occurs for adolescents who lose a parent to death" (Masterson, 2012, p. 370).*

Adolescence, a time of transition, learning oneself and experimenting with the world is a critical maturation period. This developmental stage is best progressed with support provided by parental and caring adult guidance. The loss of a parent has a seismic impact on a minor and can have an equally enormous influence on a child's sense of stability in relationships, daily life, and emotional functioning (LaFreniere & Cain, 2015). The death of a parent "is in itself a tragic, disrupting and irreversible event which leaves the child with an ongoing bereavement process as he or she develops into adulthood" (Stikkelbroek, Prinzie, de Graaf, ten Have, Cuijpers, 2012, p. 216). Thus, coping with the loss of a parent can prove to be a significant challenge during these determinative years as illustrated by Patrick Chandler, a sixteen-year-old male, performed by Lucas Hedges in the film *Manchester by the Sea*. Patrick experiences the death of his father, Joe Chandler (acted by Kyle Chandler), during his junior year of high school. At this time, Patrick is faced with grieving his father's loss, witnessing the effects of prolonged grief, and becoming exposed to the fragility of adults while desperately clinging to salvage the remainder of his youth.

The loss of a father during a child's formative years can have a significant impact on a multitude of variables within the child's life. Logistically, "parental death is likely to be succeeded by a series of life events for bereaved children.

Domestic routines will change markedly, and may well involve the change of caregivers" (Dowdney, 2000, p. 826). Emotionally, in addition to grief experienced during bereavement, "the loss of a parent during childhood often presents a cascade of difficult life changes that create new realms of stress for a bereaved child" (Lafreniere & Cain, 2015, p. 247). These changes can destabilize the level of consistency the adolescent possessed in various environments. The effects are global and may directly modify one's overall emotional functioning, one's community (i.e. academic institutions, support, and relationships), financial status, family composition, and more (LaFreniere & Cain, 2015; Rostila, Berg, Arat, Vinnerljung & Hjern, 2016). For example, "these children may have to deal with geographic relocation, loss of family income, the bereavement reactions of surrounding family members, and disruptions of stability and predictability in daily routine, not to mention the lack of a major support figure" (Lafreniere & Cain, 2015, p. 247).

Prior to the death of Joe Chandler, Patrick had an active adolescent lifestyle where he and his father appeared settled within an agreeable routine. Specifically, Patrick maintained friendships with same aged peers, and had a stable academic life in the local high school of the town of Manchester. He had female interests, was engaged on an adolescent hockey team, participated in a peer made rock band and was gainfully employed on George's boat two days a week. Subsequent to his father's death, Patrick's established life was threatened significantly as a consequence of the change in his guardianship to his uncle, Lee.

Once Patrick was informed of the death of his father, he also learned that his uncle Lee was granted guardianship of his care. Soon, in fact, moments thereafter, Patrick was provided the opportunity to observe his uncle's struggles in being able to manage and regulate his emotions. In particular, Patrick witnessed his uncle emotionally decompensate and display feelings of panic regarding being responsible for the remainder of his upbringing. When a stranger made reference to the inappropriate manner in which Lee spoke to Patrick by commenting, "Nice parenting," Patrick also viewed his uncle's verbally aggressive response as he lashed out towards the individual. In an effort to manage the situation, Patrick took the initiative to help calm Lee. Patrick instinctively adopted the supportive adult role where he expressed to his uncle the need to collect himself. Unbeknownst to Patrick, this was the first, yet would not be the last incident in which his uncle would require his support when attempting to settle into the new role as his caregiver. In particular, Patrick found himself in a similar role providing his uncle with an external superego after he had an exchange with George gauging his desire to become his guardian. Patrick responded to his uncle by confronting his behaviors and directing him to what was acceptable and what was not acceptable behavior.

Patrick's direct observations of Lee's daily emotional functioning and behaviors provided him an opportunity to descry his uncle's vulnerabilities while adopting an adult position. It is not an uncommon dynamic that the remaining caregiver for a bereaved child struggles emotionally to provide adequate care. Parents and guardians engaging with their personal grief can impair their ability to provide adequate emotional support for the surviving youth. Patrick soon became aware of his guardian's limitation that rendered him unfit to care for him in the town of Manchester. In turn, Patrick witnessed behaviors that confirmed that the stability of his life was jeopardized, and his life would continue to be redefined in unwelcomed ways by his father's death.

Though Patrick engaged with his uncle and provided him support when needed, Patrick also required emotional support coping with his feelings of grief. Many times, Patrick was able to utilize a great number of ego strengths and defenses to assist him. Because of his strengths, he was relatively able to continue his typical level of functioning while mourning. Notwithstanding, when realizing that his father's body would not be able to be buried on the day of the funeral because of the frozen ground; rather, iced to preserve, Patrick's ability to cognitively understand these logistics were intact. However, emotionally Patrick struggled to weather this reality. Verbally expressing his upset to his uncle and creating an alternative option that may have permitted for the burial were insufficient methods in calming his anxieties. Typically, Patrick's functioning appeared unaffected by his grief. However, on a quotidian night, Patrick found himself overcome and in the throw of a panic attack, dysregulated when meats fell to the floor from the freezer reminding him of his father's temporary resting place.

Of benefit, Patrick was, to the best of his ability, able to resume resemblance to his normality. Many children report that they have an attribute or talent that allows them to feel a sense of competency and enjoyment. In addition to an activity, like sport, interpersonal effectiveness has also been found to have a relevance in this arena (Brewer & Sparkes, 2011). Though Patrick participated in specific activities, he also presented as a likeable and magnetic teen. "Patrick is my favorite person," his girlfriend's mother (performed by Heather Burns) stated. Her testament to his personality was reflective of his charming appeal. His personal attributes facilitated his ability to secure a great deal of peer support, which he used to both manage and distract from his grief. His secure friendships also provided him the opportunity to continue to navigate successfully in a similar manner as an unbereft adolescent might.

Adolescents tend to "have the opportunity to receive support from peers" when one's parent(s) die(s) (Lafreniere & Cain, 2015, p. 249). In particular, when Patrick learned of his father's death, he first shared this event with his peers who expressed concern. Patrick responded by openly receiving hugs from his male hockey mates. "Simply having good relationships with peers may reduce bereavement-related symptomatology" (Lafreniere & Cain, 2015, p. 250). When he returned home from the hospital, he asked whether he could have friends to the house to visit. Patrick's two male friends and female intimate partner offered comfort; and when his male peers began to behave in an age appropriate jocular manner, making unrelated jokes, Patrick related in a similar manner; engaging in their banter as if it were a typical night and his father were alive. Adolescents "who experiences the death of a parent, has the desire for the death to be acknowledged with respect. At the same time, they do not want to be perceived by their peers as different, even if they feel different" (Masterson, 2012, p. 374).

Research also finds that females tend to provide more peer support in comparison to their male counterparts (Lafreniere & Cain, 2015). Patrick's female companion offered tenderness to Patrick, stroking his back and hair as he related to his peers. She reminded Patrick of his "gentle" nature that she compared to his father's temperament. When she viewed that others lacked mindfulness to Patrick's grief, she admonished the individual(s) and cautioned that they recall the gravity of the loss for Patrick. Lafreniere & Cain's (2015) findings revealed that when parentally bereaved children receive support from their peers; though they note preferring not to engage in conversations regarding grief; peers are likely to initiate such support. When comfort is provided, the bereaved child's response may vary by having a positive or negative response; yet most children feel that the support offered is helpful. In response to his female friend's protective nature, Patrick countered each time and stated, "I'm okay," helping her to remain calm while reassuring himself and others that his functioning was unaffected. As Masterson (2012) proposed, to best "support grieving adolescents after the death of a parent, one must have some understanding of what adolescents are feelings" and what specifically they feel they require during their time of bereavement (p. 371). It appeared most important to Patrick that he was able to continue his adolescent years in a similar fashion while residing in Manchester.

Despite remaining invested in attempting to maintain stability during this tumultuous time, at times portraying a sense of calm was challenging for Patrick. According to Brewer & Sparkes (2011) youth who have lost a parent utilize a number of skills in order to live with grief they experience. One outlet youth gravitate to include physical activity in an effort to alleviate feelings of anxiety or depression and to escape and have a distraction. Sport fosters the use of sublimation, a defense to channel unwanted feeling into behaviors that are socially acceptable, by permitting the use of aggression to express control and freedom in life. Adolescents found participating in exercise coupled with being able to share their feelings with a trusted individual most helpful in coping with grief after the loss of a parent (Masterson, 2012). When Patrick's hockey coach learned of his father's death, he granted Patrick condolences and a listening ear when needed. He confided that he too experienced the death of his father in his adolescent years and could empathize with his grief. After days passed, Patrick requested that he speak with his coach regarding his feelings. Patrick asked to reconnect with the hockey team and continue to play, and attributed his desire as, "I could really use the distraction." Though exercise can be of benefit to bereaved adolescents, his coach reminded him that hockey was not a "distraction" and encouraged him to remain "off the ice." Due to Patrick's positive and effective sociability, finding means to remain active and engaged did not pose a concern.

The abundant support Patrick held reinforced his desire to remain in Manchester while adjusting to his father's death. Financially, his father arranged for him to be cared for; yet, his death provoked an inevitable change in Patrick's family composition. Prior to his father's death, Patrick resided with his father. Historically, within the United States, mothers have been exhibited consistently as primary caregivers of children. Within the Chandler home, due to his mother's history of alcohol abuse, Patrick was primarily raised by his father with the support of his uncle. Conventionally, "as children age and investment needs changes, fathers may have increasing opportunities to provide alternative forms of care" (Shenk & Scelza, 2012, p. 550). Alternatively for Patrick, because of his absent mother within the household, he relied upon his father as his primary provider since his early childhood years. Patrick's observations of his uncle in a shocked state referred to himself as, "I was just backup". Patrick experienced his uncle's statement(s) as a rejection. He reported to his uncle, "You would do anything to try and get rid of me." When Lee reassured Patrick that his feelings were false, Patrick inevitably began to comprehend the nature of his uncle's delicate emotional state.

Despite Patrick's desire to carry on his life with little interruption, it was shared that he must relocate to the Boston area to live with his uncle. Patrick advocated for himself, noting his concern regarding maintaining stability within this time of transition. He mentioned that the move would disrupt his ability to remain within his school, be close to his friends and resume work at his place of employment. In the hopes of remaining in the care of a parent and close to Manchester to complete his education, Patrick created an alternative plan for his care. Rather than relocate with his uncle, he reported awareness of the whereabouts of his estranged mother, Elise Chandler, performed by Gretchen Mol. Though his uncle reminded him that his father would never desire him to reunite with his mother due to her past substance use, Patrick contacted his mother via email in spite of his uncle's directive. Patrick alerted his mother of his father's death and his mother reciprocated contact. She extended an invitation to reconnect with Patrick over lunch. When his mother called Patrick, his uncle disconnected the phone with her. Patrick again advocated to meet his mother; where his uncle agreed to support him.

After connecting with his mother over a meal with her husband, Patrick quickly learned that his mother was potentially less emotionally equipped to care for him than his uncle. He realized that his mother was anxious and struggled to communicate with him. Becoming overwhelmed, she excused herself from the table, where her husband checked on her, leaving Patrick at the table alone. Patrick's desire to live with his mother in a neighboring town to Manchester was further diminished once he received an email from his mother's husband who requested that all future communication be funneled through him due to his belief that his mother's emotional stability was at risk with further direct communication from him.

At the close of the film, Patrick gained acceptance that his remaining family was unable to meet his needs. His mother and his uncle were unfit caregivers though Patrick begged for Lee to continue to care for him. Lee was capable to muster the courage to communicate to Patrick that he was unable to enact what Patrick needed from him; to be "the powerful role that the surviving parent or guardian could play in a bereaved child's life" (Brewer & Sparkes, 2011, p. 286). Instead, Patrick was left to share the harsh reality that his family was unavailable to be functional adequate caregivers. In order to provide Patrick with a stable household, one that was emotionally healthy while allowing him to remain in the town of Manchester, it was decided that George would be granted guardianship over Patrick. Patrick continued to have the option to visit with his uncle in Boston when desired. This unpleasant arrangement supported Patrick's notion of, "I'm an orphan," describing his newfound state.

For Patrick, the death of his father accompanied numerous losses. Patrick's grief comprised of the loss of his father, the fantasy of an emotionally healthy uncle and a relationship with his mother. Patrick's life concluded quite interrupted; yet, secure in the town of Manchester with adopted parents and a loving caring uncle close by.

**What Makes this Character Rich?**

The character of Patrick Chandler is a teen who is found managing the emotions of experiencing three consecutive losses: the death of his father, the loss of hope that his mother was able to create and manage a relationship with him and the loss that his uncle Lee was fit to provide care for him. Despite the tremendous deficiency of capable caregivers in his life, Patrick is able to maintain a solid semblance of adolescent life.

In part, Patrick presented as an individual who used many personal strengths to manage his affect and grief. Specifically, Patrick relied upon the use of humor, a higher-level defense, in order to navigate challenging times.

According to Brewer and Sparkes (2011), adolescents in times of bereavement continue to appreciate "having fun, a sense of humour, and laughing," which are "vital resources in dealing with grief" (p. 288). Further, adolescents tend to use humor to ward emotionally challenging topics from becoming overwhelming to explore (Brewer & Sparkes, 2011). Patrick utilized the defense of humor readily. However, at times, he was posed with distressing realities that included facing the knowledge of his father's body temporary whereabouts and supporting his uncle during outbursts. In these moments, Patrick's use of humor was unavailable. Instead, he was stricken with painful affect that rapidly became overwhelming for him to manage.

Furthermore, Patrick's internal defense mechanisms were limited; an age-appropriate circumstance. When he was unable to manage his feelings and lacked internal resources to adequately cope, Patrick relied upon external supports. Specifically, to Patrick's benefit, he exhibited interpersonal skills that served him well. Though his girlfriend characterized him as a "kiss ass," he used his charm to gain likeability and strong social connections within the town. Patrick was well liked by his peers and adults alike and was well engaged in the community. He was cognizant of his ability to relate positively with others that provided him a positive self-regard and confidence in his interpersonal abilities as illustrated by his response to his uncle who asked whether the girls who ran to his car were also his girlfriends. "They wish," Patrick stated.

Because of Patrick's strengths, he was successful in being able to continue to navigate his teenage life. Bereaved adolescents note that during bereavement the goal is not recovery per se. "The emphasis was not on doing their 'grief work,' but on having fun; not finding ways to survive, but on aspiring to thrive; not simply trying to cope, but learning to live with bereavement" (Brewer &

Sparkes, 2011, p. 289). For Patrick, this manner of navigating through grief was indisputably his pursuit. He found value in the ability to have fun. He continued to have a strong desire to relate as a typical teen learning to cope with grief while investing in his relationships with friends and supportive adults.

Bereavement negatively impacts children, where they are more inclined to exhibit symptoms that are consistent with the diagnosis of depression (Cerel, Fristad, Verducci, Weller & Weller, 2006). Research indicates that after the death of a parent, bereaved children have "an increased risk of a major depressive episode" in comparison to their same aged non-bereaved peers (Gray, Weller, Fristad & Weller, 2011, p. 279). Patrick's natural temperament coupled with his supports served as protective factors that assisted him in maintaining his overall functioning.

The life of Patrick was followed for only a brief time period. The audience was not afforded the opportunity to view Patrick's functioning once transitioned into his guardian's home and adopted. We see that Patrick was able to sustain his current level of functioning at the time when the ground softened enabling for burial of his father. One is left to hypothesize regarding how the transition effected his functioning thereafter, how grief affected him once settled into a routine with his new caregiver and whether he was able to sustain the use of supports to foster his functioning. Based upon current research, one might suspect that Patrick's grief would change as time progressed. He may continue to appear well adjusted at times; and, at other times, he may appear somewhat depressed (Dowdney, 2000). Although changes in emotions can be predicted to occur with grief, Patrick determined that remaining within the town of Manchester would provide him his best chance of continuing to access supportive resources and continue his development successfully.

BEST PSYCHOLOGY IN FILM

## **RANDI CHANDLER**

Performed by: Michelle Williams

# RESOLVED

## BEST PSYCHOLOGY IN FILM

> *"Never lose hope. Storms make people stronger and never last forever."*
>
> – Roy T. Bennett

The process and challenges of grieving the death of one's children is explored within the film *Manchester by the Sea* and within the conceptualization of the character of Lee Chandler. For some, life changes as a direct result of the grief experienced. The extraordinary heartache and suffrage that occurs can be disabling. Typical life functions can become compromised. For others, time of bereavement is managed in a manner that allows one to experience the pain of grief while continuing to actively engage with progressing and evolving in life. Randi Chandler, performed by Michelle Williams, the wife of the protagonist, Lee Chandler (acted by Casey Affleck), within the film *Manchester by the Sea* is portrayed as a powerful character; one who copes and moves through the grief of the death of her three children in stark contrast to Lee Chandler's process. The impact Randi Chandler has upon framing the understanding and life of Lee Chandler is one of substantial quality. Despite the sparse quantity in which Randi presents within the film; in fact, she is found in a mere seven scenes, the juxtaposition of Randi to Lee's presentation established a worthy OSCAR® nomination for Best Supporting Actress.

Most notable, in Randi's brief presence, she performs three distinct roles. These roles included one of a wife, a mother, and a friend. Within the first scenes, Randi is depicted as sharing the roles of a wife and a mother. She is introduced as Lee's infirmed wife and the mother of his three children. Though she is found lying in the bed, when Lee enters the room, it is implied that she has cared for the children for the duration of the day while he was on a fishing trip with his brother and nephew. Though Lee attempted to make advances towards her, she declined providing gentle, yet firm boundaries reminding him that she was ill. Her role as a wife appeared to gratify both Lee and herself, as they exchanged positive interactions with banter, lighthearted frustration, and laughter.

Randi's role as a mother is further illustrated in Lee's memory of her being rescued from the burning family home. She responded in horror; yelling fearfully alerting the firefighters that her children remained in the flames, "My children are still in there! My children are still in there!" Inconsolable; she kicked and screamed as she was carried away by paramedics in an effort to prevent her from reentering the house. Morning arrives, where Randi was placed on a gurney and within an ambulance using oxygen to assist her recovery. When Lee placed his hand on her shoulder to offer comfort, her body shook, which nudged his hand off. At this time, her response as a mother after the traumatic death of her children was paramount; and her ability to respond as a wife was obstructed by the trauma she experienced.

"When death occurs, family members need to intend to be together so that their grief can be shared" (Anderson, 2010, p. 130). Within *Manchester by the Sea* the narrative of Randi does not provide specifics regarding her grieving process. Though, after years have passed, she is reintroduced once she learns of the death of Lee's brother, Jo (performed by Kyle Chandler). She called Lee to offer condolences and spoke to him gingerly; relating to him as a friend. Randi requested that she attend the services of his brother. When her request was granted, she informed Lee that she was expecting the birth of a child. Randi provided a boundary between her and her ex-husband, giving information to solidify that she had the opportunity for motherhood again; yet, the role of being a mother would no longer include him in her family.

According to research, there may be gender differences in relation to how individuals grieve. "The extremes of grief are unique and different for all. A mother might assume 'he is grieving less than I am' rather than what may actually be the case, that 'he is grieving differently'" (Stroebe and Schut, 2010, p. 282). Bereaved women are better able to access emotional resources to have better outcomes after the death of a loved one in comparison to their male counterparts (Neria & Litz, 2003). Randi's ability to grieve the loss of her children and continue to progress in her life was depicted when she arrived to the funeral accompanied by her husband. She interacted with individuals, provided customary hugs, and greeted loved ones. When she approached Lee, he appeared dejected and morose. Randi introduced her husband, hugged Lee, and began to tear. Stroebe and Schut (2010) shared that Wijngaards, et al. (2008) posited, "Women appear to be more loss-oriented following bereavement, feeling and expressing their distress at their loss; men are more restoration-oriented, actively engaging with the problems and practical issues associated with loss" (p. 282). Notably, Lee used a similar, logical, problem solving approach, specifically during the immediate time of bereavement after the death of his brother. His aloof presentation did not offer an emotional response to the reality that he faced an additional significant loss. In contrast, Randi was receptive to compassion from others that created an environment to accept condolences, and express her affective experience of grief.

Randi's connection to others and her ability to resume and maintain relationships speaks to her global interpersonal skills. In the face of pain and grief, Randi was able to maintain a relationship with her former brother-in-law.

She described that throughout the years they remained in touch and were "friends." Additionally, Randi continued to be willing to accept love in her life. Her marriage and the anticipated birth of a child provided her with a second opportunity to experience family dynamics, unconditional love, and motherhood. Despite coping with the death of her children that occurred in a traumatic way, Randi continued to remain capable of resuming and generating interpersonal relationships with others.

"As Walsh and McGoldrick rightly observe, each individual within a family will have particular grief for the unique relationship with the lost family member" (Anderson, 2010, p. 130). Randi had an opportunity to observe years after the death of their children Lee's continued acute bereaved state. Her response was one of concern. Her observations yielded evidence that Lee's grieving process contrasted hers significantly. Randi's expressed love for Lee motivated her to confront him using an empathetic approach. She shared her awareness that he struggled with feelings of sadness and with being successful in moving on with his life. "Too often, women and men alike deny their partner's pain and attempt to regulate how the other grieves" (Anderson, 2010, p. 133). However, Randi, woebegone and sobbing, implored Lee to hear her apologies for her behaviors in the past towards him. She begged for him to communicate with her his feelings regarding his emotional health; because as she described, "You can't just die. Honey. I see you walking around here." Randi was greatly pained by her ex-husband's paralysis due to grief and was unable to ignore his presentation. Challenged by her observations, she noted her inability to tolerate holding her feelings by stating, "I just got to get this out."

Randi's upset and worry regarding her ex-husband's functioning demonstrated the potential challenges she may have faced while married and coping with the grief of their children. Her ability to continue to move forward in her life suggested that there was a discrepancy between her and her ex-husband's ability to grieve the death of their children in a cohesive manner. Anderson (2010) noted, "the tasks of grieving are difficult for individuals: they are even more complicated when the family is the mourner" (p.131). "The grief families experience when loss occurs is more than the sum of individual grief and needs to be expressed in ways appropriate" (Anderson, 2010, p. 130). Within Anderson's (2010) work he noted that a family may aid in the grieving process by employing the following:

1. Acknowledging as a family the loss,
2. Sharing the affective experience and pain in an effort to build a shared narrative and memory of the deceased,
3. Reorganizing the family system considering the loss experienced;
4. Restoring meaning or faith into the family unit to foster the ability to be free to revive hope.

Randi and Lee's struggle to be able to engage in a conversation that directly addressed the past appeared to be a demonstration of residual symptomatology present when they were a couple attempting to cope together the losses of their children.

Due to the brief nature of Randi's appearance within the film, providing a comprehensive assessment of her presentation is limited. Social interactions as well as her utilized defense mechanisms were not furnished within her narrative. However, Randi's interpersonal skills were critical in understanding how her presence was of support to Lee Chandler's role. In particular, Randi was consistently portrayed as an individual who shared her thoughts and feelings readily. Whether as a wife when she expressed upset to her husband for making loud noises with friends at two in the morning while the children slept demanding that they vacate the home or as a friend when she confronted Lee regarding his prolonged grief symptoms, Randi was presented as an individual who was honest based in love. "I love you. I don't know if I'm suppose to say that," she shared with her ex-husband years after their divorce.

Affectively, Randi was insightful regarding her feelings. She was consciously aware of the conflictual emotions she experienced; and, in turn, had the ability to be transparent with her ex-husband regarding how she felt. She exhibited a range of emotions: fatigue, satisfaction, anger, horror, guilt, sadness, etc. In most scenes, her behaviors were consistent and a direct parallel to what she was feeling. The expression of her emotions was both uninhibited and authentic to her role.

**What Makes This Character Rich?**

Randi is a woman who exhibited great courage. After the death of her children and the loss of her marriage to Lee, she grieved and was able to admit to Lee, "My heart was broken, 'cause it's always going to be broken;" yet, she reengaged with the world. The sadness in which she possessed appeared to be directed towards Lee and his inability to move through his grief in a way that allowed him to be accessible to the positive and negative aspects of life.

Randi's pain was depicted when she saw that Lee continued to struggle to cope with his grief. Despite her martial status and infant child, Randi's internal love and anguish experienced for Lee evoked her to initiate a challenging emotional conversation in an effort for healing to take place. Her intense concern for Lee's wellbeing, the admission of love that she continued to have for him and the vulnerability she exhibited provided a clear illustration of an individual who, regardless to the discomfort felt in a given situation, was capable of acknowledging and expressing herself genuinely.

BEST PSYCHOLOGY IN FILM

## *MOONLIGHT*

Directed by: Barry Jenkins

## *SCENE I*

*Juan, slowly drives a blue car. His radio plays "Every Nigger is a Star". He parks the car, takes a cigarette from the box, places it in his mouth, opens the door, stands, shuts the door and places the cigarette behind his ear. Juan looks across the street. A man approaches a young man standing on the street. Juan approaches the two men talking.*

**AZU:** "Hey, my man, T., what's going on dawg?"

**TERRENCE:** "What's up, what's up?"

**AZU:** "How you doing?"

**TERRENCE:** "What yah need?"

**AZU:** "Can you help me out, man?"

**TERRENCE:** "No, I can't do it bro. Yah gotta keep it moving. I can't do it right now bro."

**AZU:** "Come on man, what you talkin' 'bout man? This is me."

**TERRENCE:** "Police out here man, keep it moving bro."

**AZU:** "Come on man…"

**TERRENCE:** "Boy, step aside.

*Juan walks closer to Terrence.*

**TERRENCE:** "What's up?"

*Juan greets Terrence by grasping his hand and pressing his shoulder against his.*

| | |
|---|---|
| **TERRENCE:** | "Hey how you doin' man?" |
| **JUAN:** | "What's good wit yah?" |
| **TERRENCE:** | "I'm alright man. Out here handlin' business as usual." |
| **AZU:** | "Look man, I don't mean no disrespect or nothin' to you, I'm just trying to see if I can just get a little…" |
| **TERRENCE:** | "Ugh, you know you can't get nothin', man. Yah know what time it is bro. I keep lookin' out for yah man…" |
| **AZU:** | "Just a little something man?" |
| **TERRENCE:** | "All my little somethin's cost a little somethin' man. If you don't got it, gotta get to steppin' nigga, you know what time it is? I don't feel like repeating myself." |
| **AZU:** | "Hey, you know you my man, right Juan?" |
| **JUAN:** | "This nigga" Juan laughs. |
| **TERRENCE:** | "Yo. Trippin', man." |
| **AZU:** | "See-see-see-see if you can do something here for me?" |

*Azu fumbles with money in his hand.*

| | |
|---|---|
| **TERRENCE:** | "What the fuck I just told you? Let me get this shit! Nigga, get the fuck up out of here, man." |

*Terrence uses two hands to grab the money from Azu's hands.*

| | |
|---|---|
| **TERRENCE:** | "Gone on! Oh, get that nigga!" he instructed a male located across the street. |

……..

| | |
|---|---|
| **TERRENCE:** | "What's up?" |
| **JUAN:** | "I'm good, good?" |

| | |
|---|---|
| **TERRENCE:** | "I'm just out here, you know." |
| **JUAN:** | "Yeah." |
| **TERRENCE:** | "Regular day. You know. It's in the cut, everybody cleaned out if you need anything." |
| **JUAN:** | "Business good?" |
| **TERRENCE:** | "Yeah, it's good. I got something fo' yah." |

*Terrence bends and begins to retrieve an item from his leg.*

| | |
|---|---|
| **JUAN:** | "No, no hold onto that. Empty the register on the weekend." |
| **TERRENCE:** | "Alright, no problem, son." |
| **JUAN:** | "How yah mom feelin' now?" |
| **TERRENCE:** | "Oh, she doing good. She doin' excellent." |
| **JUAN:** | "Better?" |
| **TERRENCE:** | "Yeah, she doin' better, yah know." |
| **JUAN:** | "She's in my prayers, man. Peace." |
| **TERRENCE:** | "Most naturally. Thank you." |

*Juan shakes hands and brings Terrence close to his shoulder.*

| | |
|---|---|
| **TERRENCE:** | "Thanks for the opportunity, I'm out here." |

*Juan begins to walk away and sees five boys run across the street chasing a young boy with a blue backpack.*

| | |
|---|---|
| **YOUNG BOYS:** | "Get him! Get your ass right here. Get him! Why you always runnin'? Goin' around with that faggot ass, bro! Ain't gonna catch him! Kick his ass!" |

BEST PSYCHOLOGY IN FILM

*IDENTITY*

> *"Sleep my little baby-oh*
> *Sleep until you waken*
> *When you wake you'll see the world*
> *If I'm not mistaken....*
> *Kiss a lover*
> *Dance a measure*
> *Find your name*
> *And buried treasure...*
> *Face your life*
> *Its pain,*
> *Its leisure,*
> *Leave no path untaken."*
> – Neil Gaiman

> *"When I discover who I am, I'll be free."*
> – Ralph Ellison

Living day-to-day, managing responsibilities, and engaging with others can leave little time to process and integrate new experiences into how one thinks and feels about oneself. Having an understanding of one's identity is a lifetime journey. Aspects of the self changes and are refined through childhood, adolescence, and adulthood years. The roles and responsibilities at various points in a lifespan also changes and requires one to continuous self-adjust. With maturity, the way one understands oneself and behaves can change significantly. Various people such as family, supportive adults, peers, and friends influence both our perceptions of ourselves and who we ultimately become. For some, the process of learning and maintaining one's identity comes with apparent ease. However, "human identity is a complex process" that is "constantly evolving" (Marquez, 2014, 143). As such, for others, learning and accepting oneself may be riddled with challenges and conflicts. Within the film *Moonlight*, directed by Barry Jenkins, stages of early–psychological identity development of the protagonist "Little", "Chiron," and "Black" were observed through life shaping experiences.

Little, performed by Alex Hibbert, was introduced as a youngster mocked, ostracized, and bullied by his peers. His working mother's ability to meet his needs was compromised due to her substance abuse, which made home life a lonely existence. Comfort found Little randomly whilst running away from the taunts of his peers into a crack house. Juan, acted by Mahershala Ali, a concerned drug dealer, invited him to his home with his girlfriend, Teresa performed by Janelle Monae. Initially, Little used a cautious approach when interacting with the couple. Over time, he generated a solid reliable relationship, where their home became a surrogate safe house when in need of solace.

Additionally, Juan adopted a father figure role in Little's life and Teresa became an alternate maternal figure who validated his experience. Upon the path of developing one's identity, individuals wish "to be recognized, dignified and esteemed by others. It is our human dignity which is at stake" (Marquez, 2014, p. 148).

In childhood, "regulating the distress associated with negative social events, in addition to other negative stimuli, is important in self-concept development" (Sebastian, Burnett, Blakemore 2008, p. 444). Little failed continuously to successfully manage his distressed emotions. As a child, Little had limited power to resolve the negative interactions he encountered with his mother. Additionally, he lacked skills to be able to relate to his same-aged peers. Consequently, such tumultuous interactions persisted well into Little's adolescent years. The result of these hostile relationships negatively impacted his self-concept, confidence, and self-esteem.

"Adolescence is a particular important time for self-concept to be shaped by other people, especially peers" (Sebastian, et al., 2008, p. 444). Within his teenage years, Little ensured that others referred to him as "Chiron," his legal name. Chiron, acted by Ashton Sanders, coped with his chronic stressors by using internalization, the process of holding feelings inward rather than readily expressing emotion(s). When approached and physically attacked, instead of fleeing from the conflict as he did as a child, Chiron often surrendered to the assaults without attempting to defend himself. "By early adolescence, children are more likely to compare themselves with others and to understand that others are making comparisons and judgments about them; they also begin to place higher value on these judgments" (Sebastian, et al. 2008, p. 441). During these formative years, when one attempts to perceive themselves through the understanding that one offers, what one will see are distortions and one's unique self with one's beauty will be marred and viewed as unattractive (O'Donohue, 1997). Chiron faced such consequences. He felt that others perceived him as a vulnerable, defenseless victim; one who was worthy of bullying and physical assaults. He silently obliged this perception by acquiescing to their verbal and physical brutality.

Chiron's trajectory of global identity development followed an unconventional path. Since childhood, he experienced little validation regarding his identity that would build a positive self-esteem. Instead, Chiron witnessed his mother's addiction cause her to be unavailable; worsening the mother-child relationship over time. Further, he remained a target of ridicule and physical abuse from his peers and relied upon the acceptance from an occasional accepting peer, Kevin (performed by Jharrel Jerome) and Teresa after Juan's death.

> The experience of terror and disempowerment during adolescence effectively compromises the three normal adaptive tasks of this stage of life: the formation of identity, the gradual separation from the family of origin, and the exploration of a wider social world (Herman, 1992, p. 61).

Possibilities within Chiron's environment lacked promise, where incarceration and death were likely known options. Connecting with Kevin, and ultimately engaging in his first sexual encounter, illustrated for Chiron that validation, connection, and intimacy were possible occurrences with peers. Kevin continued to refer to Chiron by the nickname "Black" and an intimacy emerged. Thereafter, Chiron adopted the moniker of Black, and Chiron's identity was again altered. Consequently, his last depicted act as Chiron included his newfound ability to express his emotion of anger towards his bully and made it known that he was willing to fight back and wrestle for his dignity.

Within adulthood, Black adopted the identity of the only familiar and engaged male figure known to him, Juan. "Little" and the thin build of "Chiron" were abandoned for a tall, muscular man. Similarly to Juan, Black secured employment as a neighborhood drug dealer. Black's identification with Juan suggested that he internalized Juan's attributes, which fostered his ability to become comparable to him in physical form and behavior. The process of identification is customary during an individual's maturation and "can serve nondefensive functions in normal development" (Gabbard, 2005, p. 36). Yet, Black was aware that Juan navigated romantic relationships in a manner that would require him to divert from Juan's path. This would require Black to discontinue emulating Juan and find courage to embrace his genuine self.

Upon revisiting a source of his childhood pain, Black experienced a tender moment with his mother. Apologies for past hurts were provided and a resolution and healing began. Once receiving validation from his mother, Black became sufficiently confident to explore and seize his personal desires independent of concerns and judgments of others. Black travelled with hope to reconnect with someone who previously was capable of providing him with similar acceptance, Kevin (adult), performed by Andre Holland. When Kevin saw Black, he found that Black had been transformed and commented, "It's not what I expected" and stated, "It's not you" as he took account for how Black presented. Kevin noticed and acknowledged for Black that the individual with whom he best identified with, Juan, did not accurately represent his true self. Black's expression of his identity, though challenged by Kevin, did not dissuade Black from continuing to pursue his individual desires. Previously, such an interaction that questioned any aspect of himself or identity may have caused Black to retreat; however, the significance of the validation he obtained from his mother fostered his capacity to offer himself to Kevin and share affections with him. Once accepted by Kevin, Black's ability to be demonstrative of his true self was further reassured, where he could feel safe to enter a mutually reciprocal intimate relationship.

Palahniuk (1999) noted that one's entire being lacks originality; rather, one is a combination of the investment of each person known. Events and interactions that shape one's identity require time to integrate. These experiences are significant and influences perceptions and behaviors in life.

When life moves quickly, taking time to recognize who one has become can be challenging. At times, awareness of oneself can be accompanied by a mixture of feelings; loss of whom one once were and feelings of empowerment and victory based upon who one has become. Embracing that identity is not fixed, rather is an element of ourselves that is ever evolving, allows changes in the sense of self to become welcomed, healthy occurrences during life.

BEST PSYCHOLOGY IN FILM

## *JUAN*

Performed by: Mahershala Ali

BEST PSYCHOLOGY IN FILM

*SHAME*

> *"There is a face beneath this mask, but it isn't me.
> I'm no more the face than I am the muscles beneath it,
> or the bones beneath that."*
> – Steve Moore

> *"I realize then that it's not enough to know what someone is called.
> You have to know who they are."*
> – Gayle Forman

Humans vary in numerous ways. Similar to snowflakes, no two are exactly alike. We are unique, and the complexity of any given individual is infinite. A person may appear a specific way in their manner. However, there may exist endless idiosyncratic undercurrents that contrast the nature in which the person presents. As humans, we find comfort in scanning our environment and the people within it to generate rapid conclusions that summarize and prepare us to navigate the environment with efficiency. In using such approach, we can simply miss specific information that provides an opportunity to gather a rich understanding of our surroundings and with whom we share our lives. Juan, performed by Mahershala Ali, visually demonstrates the characterological diversity found within one's individual disposition.

Opening, Juan was found interacting with his employee, Terrence, performed by Shariff Earp, standing in a neighborhood of public housing. As Terrence engaged with his client, Juan observed and provided him space to conduct a transaction. Juan was a local illegal drug distributor with Terrence working under his business. When Juan reengaged with Terrence, Juan inquired regarding the health of Terrence's mother and his life, "She doing better? She's in my prayers." Although engagement with Terrence took the form of a concerned person, Juan also enacted the role of a stern employer. Juan ensured that Terrence remained aware of his position and later scolded him for allowing clients to "freebase at the spot" which could bring attention to their business practices; thus placing future transactions in jeopardy with the law.

Given Juan's initial presentation, one may summarize his character relying upon a vast number of stereotypes ascribed to drug dealers. Prior to forming a crystalized concept of him, the process is interrupted by children running intrusively through the scene of Juan and Terrence. A fearful child, Little, acted by Alex R. Hibbert, was glimpsed being chased by a group of peers. Juan responded to the commotion with curiosity and found Little hiding in an abandoned building, a crack house, after the children departed the grounds. Juan attempted to build a rapport with Little, noting his concern for his safety. Because Little presented as shy and unwilling to share with Juan his name or the location of his home, Juan provided time to invest in him. Juan articulated, "I can't just have you running around these dopeholes." After a meal, and making no further progress into knowing more about him, Juan took the responsibility to transport the reluctant Little to his residence, introduced him to his girlfriend and welcomed him into his home. Once learning where Little resided, Juan drove him to his home safely. The contrast in Juan's character of his professional self: a drug dealer that supported other drug dealers' careers and his personal self: a concerned citizen who inconvenienced himself to care for a child can be difficult to reconcile. Somehow, the care that he provided Little presides and the earlier presentation that included his profession fades into the vista along with feelings that may be evoked from such knowledge. Juan's character is silently redeemed where he embodied the role of a likeable, kind volunteering male to fulfill a neglected role in a needy child's life.

Juan's continued engagement with Little emerged when he arrived home to find Little sitting upon a chair in his front lawn. Rather than bring him to his home, Juan drove him to the beach. He confided in Little about his youth in Cuba and educated him regarding African American people in the world. Juan encouraged Little to create his own identity independent from the contributions others may desire for him. "No one can make that decision for you," Juan informed regarding determining his future self. At the beach, Juan taught Little to swim, an illustrative metaphor for being able to navigate through rough tides that he might encounter in the future.

The two roles in which Juan encapsulated, one of a drug dealer and one as a nurturing father figure to a wanting child continued to be reinforced. Juan's level of discord in which he experienced as a result of these differences in his attributes appeared minimum until others found it challenging to integrate the discrepancies. Instead of viewing Juan as a complex individual, he became viewed by others as a hypocrite. "Who the hell you think you is?" Little's mother (Paula, performed by Naomie Harris) confronted. Intoxicated by the use of Juan's product, Paula stated that he had no right to judge her drug addiction and parenting because he was the individual responsible for her supply. In this moment, Paula held a mirror to Juan revealing to him the reality of their relationship to one another. Juan was not a man who cared for her son in its entirety; there was no mistaking that their relationship was significantly more complex. His profession, and consequently, his behaviors, led to a different conclusion: he was a drug dealer and she was his customer. As a result, the two aspects of Juan that he regularly enacted could no longer continue to go unnoticed and unacknowledged.

When an individual possesses dichotomous qualities, assimilating the diversity of information can be difficult for individuals who interact with the person and for the person him/herself. The quantity of features that is required to integrate into the understanding of one's character equally influences the quality of comfort one has with possessing a range of behaviors that appear contradictory. Further, the level of personal acceptance of these differences also impact how variances are experienced with the self and with others. Individuals who struggle to integrate varied personal roles and behaviors that qualitatively present as fundamental personality differences can be inclined to experience emotional dissonance, a level of discomfort that arises due to the difference between what is actual and what is desired. When this occurs, one can become susceptible to experiencing feelings of guilt and shame regarding their behaviors and who they are.

Historically, researchers and persons alike have struggled to locate differences between the experience of shame and guilt. Shame and guilt are frequently referred to interchangeably. In fact, shame and guilt are similar where they "are both self-conscious emotions that arise from self-relevant failures and transgressions, but they differ in their object of evaluation" (Tangney, Stuewig & Martinez, 2014, p. 799). When an individual experiences feelings of guilt, one tends to feel "tension, remorse and regret" (Tangney, et al., 2014, p. 799). One experiences dysphoric feelings regarding their behavior that lead the individual to partake in corrective action. However, "in common parlance, shame is a negative, crisis emotion closely connected with disgrace" (Scheff, 2000, p. 97). For one to experience feelings of shame, one must possess a "self-critical and sophisticated self-consciousness which relies on the concept of another such that in this sophisticated self-consciousness one realizes the discrepancy of his/her own assumptions about his/her actual action or state" (Dost & Yagmurlu, 2008, p. 110). In turn, "feelings of shame involve a painful focus on the self—'I am a bad person'—whereas feelings of guilt involve a focus on a specific behavior-I did a bad thing" (Tangney, et al., 2014, p. 799).

Once Juan hears Paula's account of their relationship, sentiments described by Tanger, et al. (2014) are actively present within the scene. Being confronted by Paula regarding his choices, he seemingly experienced tension and regret. Paula made reference to Juan's character by stating, "You ain't shit," suggesting that he was a bad person. Using theory, one might anticipate that he may respond with feelings of shame. Yet, Juan seemed to interpret her conceptualization of him as, I have done a bad thing. By having a connection to her drug use, this behavior ensued guilt; for, he did not attribute this connection to make him a "bad person".

"Guilt motivates the individual to repair the harm he/she caused" (Dost & Yagmurla, 2008, p. 122). Within *Moonlight* Juan's motivations for caring for Little was unknown. The closeness that they shared was palpable. The nurturance that Juan provided Little secured him with a safe place to openly question and explore his sexuality. The accepting environment also enabled Little to directly inquire regarding Juan's profession, "You sell drugs?" he asked. Once receiving an honest affirmative response, Little confirmed with Juan his belief of his mother's substance use: "My mother uses drugs?" he asked linking Juan's work to his mother's condition, a neglectful mother. With an understanding between Juan and Little that Juan's employment supported his mother's drug addiction, Juan became unable to look Little in his eyes; and was rendered ashamed.

> When people feel shame about the self, they feel diminished, worthless and exposed….rather than motivating reparative action, the acutely painful shame experience often motivates a defensive response. When shamed, people want to escape, hide, deny responsibility and blame other people (Tangney, et al., 2014, p. 799).

Other negative feelings tend to accompany shame including, "embarrassment, humiliation…. that involves reactions to rejection or feelings of failure or inadequacy" (Scheff, 2000, p. 96). Though shame may prompt paralysis, it can equally elicit "prosocial motives" (Tangney, et al., 2014, p. 803) that promote one to have a desire to make reparations and ask for forgiveness. "Most theorists agree that moral failures are painful mainly because a failure is taken as a sign that the self suffers a serious defect" (Gausel, Vignoles & Leach, 2016, p. 134). For Juan, Little's perspective of his responsibility; and, at the very least, his complicity of his mother's addiction caused him to withdraw in his shame. In response, Juan remained at the table after Little rose and walked away. Juan was unable to motivate himself to repair Little's perceptions of him. He was unable to move; stilled by the confrontation and overwhelming sense of disesteem.

In life "…we must all deal with moral failure, at least occasionally. People often experience feelings of shame as a result of their failures" (Gausel, et al., 2016, p. 118). Once Little became a teen (referred to as Chiron, performed by Ashton Sanders), it was learned that Juan had died. Little's earlier disappointments in Juan's choice of profession resulted in a failure to actualize the ideal role model for him. In the absence of Juan in his life, Teresa carried the role Juan was successfully able to establish; a reliable caregiver. His commitment to Little provided a legacy of securing basic needs, a stable shelter of love and encouragement and a view of the complexities of individuals who are both honorable and flawed.

**What Makes This Character Rich?**

Juan's character propels the audience to consider the elaborative nature of an individual's character. The qualities of Juan encourage questions of whether we are what we do, whether someone who does bad things can be good and how to integrate discrepancies in one's presentation. If Juan were a law-abiding citizen performing legal activities and providing mentorship to Little, the intricacy of his personality would possibly present as unidimensional. Providing the contrast of his profession to how he presents personally with Little, as a father figure, contributed remarkably to the wealth of texture of his character.

Interpersonally, Juan was seen able to generate and maintain relations with others. He had a steady girlfriend who lived with him and a consistent employee. A test of his social skills presented with the success of Little. Juan was able to communicate with him despite the sensitivity of the topic. This open communication helped Little share delicate concerns he had about himself and his life.

Further, Juan's vulnerability to Little was striking. In response to his concern for Little's safety and the quality of his upbringing, Juan answered with altruism. Altruism, a sophisticated defense that enables one to commit "oneself to the needs of others over and above one's own needs" (Gabbard, 2005, p. 37), greatly influenced the support that Juan provided. Thus, it is not surprising that the disappointment Little felt in Juan for his profession evoked shame in him.

In concert to the duality of Juan's presentation, such duplicity also existed in the manner he coped with challenges that arose. Juan frequently utilized the higher order defense of altruism when experiencing positive emotional affect. When emotionally injured by feelings of shame, he solicited the use of withdrawal, a primitive defense (Gabbard, 2005) that causes one to isolate rather than connect and create resolution with others. Ego injuries for Juan caused regressions in his emotional functioning commonly found among individuals coping with difficult feelings.

Despite Juan's flaws, his character, both complex and abundant, casted lasting impressions upon Little. As an adult, Little referred to himself as "Black" (acted by Trevante Rhodes). During adulthood, Black was found aspiring to project the persona of Juan, where he presented as a muscle-bound drug distributor who drove a car with an exact ornament on the dash. At a quick glance, one may have perceived Black to be Juan rather than the male who Juan helped raise. The compelling presence Juan bestowed upon this child in need left audiences with a beloved character.

BEST PSYCHOLOGY IN FILM

## *PAULA*

Performed by: Naomie Harris

BEST PSYCHOLOGY IN FILM

*ADDICTION*

> *"No one else will ever know the strength of my love for you. After all, you're the only one who knows the sound of my heart from the inside."*
> – Kristen Proby, *Fight with Me*

Within the film *Moonlight*, Paula, performed by Naomie Harris, depicts a mother struggling with substance abuse. Within psychological research, data is scarce pertaining to the inner psychic experience of substance misusers. However, data is prolific that explores the impact the use of illicit substances have upon the nature of parenting and the consequence substance abuse has upon the relationship between parent and child; and more specifically, between mother and child. Paula, the mother of the young male protagonist (Little, Chiron & Black), is illustrated possessing two main relationships; the engagement she had with her son and the relationship she had with addiction.

"Addiction is a complex, multidimensional, multi-factorial phenomenon in which bio, psycho, social, familial, and environmental factors are implicated" (Smith & Estefan, 2014, p. 421-422). As such, the addiction of one family member can influence a broad terrain of family dynamics and significantly impact individual family members. No family system is the same; yet as addiction becomes increasingly severe, the manner in which members of the family responds to the addiction grows (Smith & Estefan, 2014). Smith and Estefan (2014) described within their literature that addressed substance misusing adolescents that responses to a family member's addiction can manifest in a myriad of unique ways. These include developing "a complex and shared system, which supports dysfunctional behaviors, enables the unchallenged addict, and constricts the family's functioning as a unit" (p. 426). Similarly, these family dynamics can be equally applicable to situations when the parent is a substance misuser. Given the

> complexities of addiction and co-occurring disorders, and the ways in which they influence parenting and the parent-child relationship, it is imperative to understand how they contribute to children's cognitive, social, and emotional developmental risk and subsequently, the best ways to intervene at a dyadic level in order to positively impact these outcomes (Paris, Herriott, Holt & Gould 2015, p. 207).

Kroll (2004) posited that it can be challenging to gain a better understanding of these factors because "we know very little about their lives as, for various reasons, their voices are rarely heard" (p. 129). What has been observed within research includes from

> both children's and adults' accounts, there was far more material in relation to parental alcohol use than to drug use, for obvious reasons. Although alcohol-related behavior will be judged and labeled, it does not carry with it the same kind and level of stigma associated with illegality and the stereotype of the drug user that pervade much of public thinking (Kroll, 2004, p. 131).

Further, according to Paris and colleagues (2015) "not all mothers who are in recovery or actively using express or demonstrate significant difficulties with parent-child interactions" (p. 208). Mothers in recovery of misusing substances "may have an impaired ability to read the child's cues" and are "unable to imagine her child's emotional or cognitive experience and thereby miss important cues or misunderstand the impact of frightening situations for the young child, such as witnessing domestic violence or substance abuse" (Paris, et al., 2015, p. 207 & 214). As a result, a "loss of childhood was a theme in several of the studies" (Kroll, 2004, p. 133).

Within *Moonlight* the parent-child relationship that Paula has with her young son, Little, depicted a relationship that was woven with complexities. In particular, Paula's parenting of Little was illustrated by displays of inconsistent and varying levels of concern for his wellbeing and development. Initially, Paula was shown walking quickly to the front door to greet her son who knocked to enter. She was concerned because he returned after being absent from the home overnight where she had no knowledge of his whereabouts. Approaching him, she asked several times, "What happen, hun? What happened, Chiron? Why you didn't come home like you 'spose to, hun?" When she learned from the adult, (Juan), who had her son in his care what occurred the previous night, she described that her son could typically "take care of himself, he good that way." Paula's statement regarding her son's ability to care for himself indicated that she allowed her elementary school-aged child to be charged with a lack of parental monitoring. The independence that she granted him was suggestive that Paula, nor another supportive adult, was physically available to Little; which, in turn, could create missed opportunities to provide him with the support he required. Though not always being readily available to Little, Paula attempted to protect her son from strangers. When Juan bid Little farewell after safely returning him home, Paula placed Little behind her, shielding him from further interactions.

Thereafter, the beginnings of Paula's substance use and the impact misuse had on her global functioning and parenting skills was quickly observed in following scenes. As noted, Little was frequently required to care for himself in an apartment that lacked resources. When home, Paula's desire to protect her son from unknown individuals diminished. In fact, she brought male friends to the home to engage in substance use. As Paula's addiction worsened, she increasingly became a stranger to her son and was equally unable to emotionally protect him from herself. Additionally, her ability to manage emotions crumbled. She responded in anger when faced with her son's look of disappointment, hurt and sadness when he watched her scurry to her bedroom to use drugs rather than care for him. In response, rather than connect and comfort him, she yelled, "don't look at me!" in her compromised state, creating a traumatic interaction that haunted Little's conscious thoughts and dreams for decades to come.

Substance dependence and addiction "impact the development of trust and the critical secure base inherent in the attachment relationship, thereby affecting the parent-child relationship in both broad and nuanced ways" (Paris, et al., 2015, p. 208). Many times, children "effectively disappeared in their own right because their lives were dominated by the needs and feelings of the parents" (Kroll, 2004, p. 134). Personal needs are ignored or neglected and the parent-child relationship exists in the presence of a third powerful influence: addiction. Addiction can be pernicious; thereby polluting healthy parent-child interactions. It takes the parent away from nurturing the parent-child relationship and leaves an absent parent. In the face of this dynamic, "substance misuse and its consequences often lead to parental separation, and children experienced a range of emotions in relation to this" (Kroll, 2004, p. 134). Fears of being left, questions of whether the substance misusing parent will return and whether they remain alive can infect children's thoughts. Yet, exposing intoxicated states to children can have equal, if not longer lasting inflictions of harm. Kroll (2014) found that "for some children, parental separation was clearly a relief from conflict and violence" (p. 134). As a result, the parent's presence and their absence can have equal traumatizing effects upon a child.

Paula's presence during the course of her son's formative years was riddled with behaviors of both addiction and love. Once dependent upon substances, Paula's impulse was to use. At times, in order to meet the needs of her addiction she demanded that her son, "find somewhere for you to be" and physically assaulted him to steal money from his pockets. Yet, a sliver of Paula's love for her son tended to find a way to shine through the turmoil. Despite her intoxicated stupors, she noticed when he was late to school, instructed that he attend and incoherently reported, "You my child!", "You are my only." while lying down embracing his hand placed on her chest. Whether present or absent, equipped or ill equipped to maintain a consistent healthy parent-child interaction, intoxicated or sober; the parent-child relationship continue to develop in the presence of those wrestling with addiction. Albeit the influence in which addiction affects the parent-child relationship is variable, consequences are experienced for all who are exposed.

### What Makes This Character Rich?

Throughout the course of the film, Paula's demonstrative affectionate nature toward her son waxed and waned. There are times where the love she had for Little/Chiron/Black was displayed clearly. For example, at the onset of the film, once Paula scolded Little for not coming home and spending the night with a stranger, she was forgiving, loving and corrective towards him. When he proceeded to attempt to engage in electronics upon his return, she directed him to read a book as an alternative behavior. Yet, following encounters depicted a stark difference in her ability to attune to her son. For instance, Little was seen knocking on the apartment door. Paula quickly opened the door, allowed him to enter and rapidly closed the door. Thereafter, she did not make time for greetings nor inquire regarding his whereabouts, as he returned home late, after dark. She rushed a male companion to join her in a back room, presumably to use substances. Similar polarized dynamics of being loving and dismissive, concerned and unavailable, connected yet abandoning persisted within the parent-child relationship exhibited. Paula's presentation of an addicted single mother elucidated the inconsistencies and unpredictability that can be experienced in the home of substance misusers.

Further, Paula's presence, personality, mothering, and behaviors that included addiction were overwhelmingly meaningful to the tone of the film, the development of the characters and the interpersonal dynamics illustrated. Equal to her presence, Paula's means of coping with stressors, by the use of escapism into substance use, resulted in a physical absence in the household. Her absence strongly influenced the landscape of the narrative as well as the quality of the character's lives around her. For example, Paula's young son walked into an empty home. He warmed water on the stove, placed the water in the tub and squirted dish liquid to add bubbles. As he sat, soaked and placed bubbled water over his face, the silence within the home magnified his solitude. And, though alone within his home; Paula's absence enormously filled the scene, where it feels irresponsible not to ask; "Where is Paula?" Assumptions of her at work (she arrives home in hospital scrubs), or fantasies of her falling deeper into addiction occupied the space when watching her son in his reclusiveness. Paula's absence provided "no source of safety or support" to her son (Kroll, 2004, p. 135). Her lack of ability to sustain hot water in the home, and the roaches trapped in the plastic covers of the florescent lights illustrated a lapse in home maintenance which was understood to be caused by neglect; a consequence of her drug addiction. And, as a result, her son was left to manage his care and the myriad of thoughts and feelings he possessed independently (Kroll, 2004).

> Despite the fact that children can be surprising resilient in the face of adversity, and that it is tempting to rely on this in a range of situations, children have their limits and it is clear that, for many children of substance misusing parents, these limits are sorely tested (Kroll, 2004, p. 137).

Once Paula was in recovery for her addiction and stable, she was able to return to making decisions that were in her best interest. She noted, "this is home," referring to the substance rehabilitation center. She accepted that her opportunity to maintain her sobriety was dependent upon her decision to help others in recovery and remain in rehabilitation.

Subsequent to her recover, Paula was able to make peace with her son, an adult man referred to as Black. "Apart from disbelief and feelings of betrayal and not being cared about, children often expressed rage, anger, and murderous feelings towards" their substance misusing parents (Kroll, 2004, p. 135). Paula's attempt to share desires for him evoked an infuriated response in Black. To be persuasive, she demanded that he attend and listen to her, where he responded, "To who ma? Hun? To you? Really though?" Similarly to many children of substance misusers, Black felt that his mother "had forfeited any right to have authority over" him "and the balance of power shifted as a consequence" (Kroll, 2004, p. 136) within their relationship.

Once the conflict between Paula and Black subsided, she was able to articulate the love that she possessed for him. She was able to own that she was unavailable when he needed her the most. She admitted that she did not provide the love he needed as a child. In her confession, she vulnerably described the possible consequences that may have resulted due to her compromised parenting. She feared that based upon her behaviors; her son may not love her. During Paula's time of substance abuse her relationship with her son deteriorated to a state where rebuilding the relationship required her to provide him with an expression of her support and unconditional love. Within Paula's final scenes, with difficulty, she was able to become the present mother that her son desperately needed.

"Addiction is an individual neuro-chemical disease, yet addiction is also occurring in a familial and social context that creates different kinds of complexities" (Smith & Estefan, 2014, p. 431). "Substance dependency is considered a disease not just of the individual but also of the family" (Smith & Estefan, 2014, p. 429). Due to the significant impact substance abuse has upon the misuser and interpersonal dynamics with family members, addiction is unable to be conceptualized within a bubble where the only individual affected is the substance misuser. Paula's substance dependency and the manner in which her addiction influenced her relationship with her son was a sobering influential hallmark to this cinematic Academy Award® winning film for Best Picture.

BEST PSYCHOLOGY IN FILM

## *FINAL THOUGHTS*

> *"Film as dream, film as music. No art passes our conscience in the way film does, and goes directly to our feelings, deep down into the dark rooms of our souls."*
>
> – Ingmar Bergman

Reflecting upon the journey taken within the previous pages, that included screening films, pontificating regarding present psychological themes, and becoming familiar with current psychological literature pertaining to aspects highlighted within ACADEMY AWARD® nominated films was a transformative process. Over the years, I found that having an interest in cinema and psychology can promote discussion to transpire and foster the passion to watch movies to better understand the impact the spoken verses have upon the characters and the global theme of the work. Being receptive to the illustration of psychological dynamics found within cinema while becoming familiar with current literature that directly address many of the concepts displayed elicited a new layer of spirited conversation. I believe Best Psychology in Film is a culmination of said conversations.

In 2017, recognized films brought cinematic work that varied tremendously in content. From conceptualizing how we use and process language and interact with those unfamiliar to us (*Arrival*), to remaining committed to one's convictions (*Hacksaw Ridge*), navigating poverty (*Hell or High Water*) and honoring the brilliant minds of those who came before us

(*Hidden Figures*); we were able to witness individuals who embodied characters that shaped our understanding of space voyages that once were believed impossible and build empathy for those who share our world who possess both similarities and differences.

Further, audiences were offered the opportunity to observe with meticulous examination the complexity and impact that both bereavement (*Manchester By the Sea*) and disappointment (*Fences*) can have upon family systems. We accompanied those who came into their identities; whether by discovering the intricacy of the adoptive family (*Lion*) or restoring a mother-child bond after enduring chronic neglect and trauma (*Moonlight*). Additionally, screening elucidated journeys of those in quest for learning oneself during the coming of age in the newly recognized developmental phase: emerging adulthood (*La La Land*). Within this body of art coupled with literature, viewers were provided means to wrestle with complex subject matters while challenging one's prior established perceptions and beliefs.

Today, as this book comes to a close, the release of the 2018 nominations has been revealed. The beginning buzz of the 90th ACADEMY AWARDS® has arrived. Inquiry regarding whether individuals will tune in, attend privately held parties, and dress in their best while watching is asked. Predictions regarding who will win specific awards; and in what category, fill the atmosphere. Due to the acclaim nominations warrant, specific films grant additional screenings to welcome patrons for a first or returning view to experience the extraordinary theme, score, and actor performances. For those who were able to enjoy the film during the first release, once nominated, individuals find themselves using an increased critical eye while enjoying a second, third, even a fourth and fifth screening to be dazzled, saddened, inspired; and, at times, changed forever.

Within the introduction of this book, I suggest the marriage of psychology and film. For those who leave the theater and possess a wonderment for the behaviors of the characters, question whether a difference of events might have altered the trajectory of the course of the character's lives, ponder upon the script and plot and experience film as more than pure entertainment; I am hopeful that Best Psychology in Film has offered an environment to invite one to become engrossed and relish in such thoughts. With an interest in the field of psychology and exceptional cinematic works available, these conversations can continue to come alive and be met with great enthusiasm.

BEST PSYCHOLOGY IN FILM

# *REFERENCES*

Albert, S. M. (2002). Anthropology and the second 50 years. *Current Anthropology,* 43(2), 338-340.

American Psychiatric Association. (2013). *Diagnostic and Statistical Manual of Mental Disorders (5$^{th}$ Edition).* Washington DC: Author.

Anderson, H. (2010). Common grief, complex grieving. *Pastoral Psychology,* 59, 127-136.

Angella, M. (2016). Work, recognition and subjectivity: Relocating the connection between work and social pathologies. *European Journal of Social Theory,* 19(3) 340-354.

Aquino, K., Douglas, S. (2003). Identity threat and antisocial behavior in organizations: The moderating effects of individual differences, aggressive modeling, and hierarchical status. *Organizational Behavior and Human Decision Processes,* 90, 195-208.

Arnett, Jeffrey, J. (2007). Suffering, selfish, slackers? Myths and reality about emerging adults. *Journal of Youth Adolescence,* 36, 23-29.

Arnett, Jeffrey, J. (2000). Emerging adulthood: A theory of development from the late teens through the twenties. *American Psychologist,* 55(5), 469-480.

Arnett, Jeffrey, J. (2007). Emerging adulthood: What is it, and what is it good for? *Society for Research in Child Development,* 1(2), 68-73.

Baumeister, R. F., Smart, L., Boden, J. M. (1996). Relation of threatened egotism to violence and aggression: The dark side of high self-esteem. *Psychological Review,* 103(1), 5-33.

Bennett, R.T. (2016). *The Light in the Heart: Inspirational Thoughts for Living Your Best Life.* Amazon Books.

Blatt, V., Ogaki, M. & Yagucki, Y. (2015). Normative behavioural economics based on unconditional love and moral virtue. *The Japanese Economic Review,* 66(2), 226-246.

Bloom, P.B.N. (2013). The public compass: Moral conviction and political attitudes. *American Politics Research,* 41(6), 937-964.

Boelen, P.A. (2016). Improving the understanding and treatment of complex grief: an important issue for psychotraumaology. *European Journal of Psychotraumatology.*

Boelen, P.A. & Huntjens, R.J.C. (2008). Intrusive images in grief: An exploratory study. *Clinical Psychology and Psychotherapy,* 15, 217-226.

Boelen, P.A., Prigerson, H.G. (2012). Commentary on the inclusion of persistent complex bereavement-related disorder in DSM-5. *Death Studies,* 36, 771-794.

Bogensperger, J & Lueger-Schuster, B. (2014). Losing a child: Finding meaning in bereavement. *European Journal of* Psychotraumatology, 5, 1-9.

Boss, P. & Carnes, D. (2012). The myth of closure. *Family Process,* 51(4), 456-469.

Bowlby, J. (1980). *Attachment and Loss. Vol. 3.* New York, NY. Basic Books.

Box Office Mojo. (2016). Retrieved from www.boxofficemojo.com.

Braslow, M.D., Guerrettaz, J., Arkin, R.M., Oleson, K.C. (2012). Self-doubt. *Social and Personality Psychology Compass,* 6, 470-482.

Breakey, H. (2016). Compromise despite conviction: Curbing integrity's moral dangers. *Journal of Value Inquiry,* 50, 613-629.

Brenner, C. (1982). *The Mind in Conflict.* International Universities Press. Connecticut.

Brewer, J.D. & Sparkes, A.C. (2011). Young people living with parental bereavement: Insights from an ethnographic study of a UK childhood bereavement service. *Social Science & Medicine,* 7, 283-290.

Bronstein, C. (2015). The analyst's disappointment: An everyday struggle. *JAPA,* 63(3), 1173-1192.

Carroll, P.J., Arkin, R.M. & Shade, C.K. (2011). Possible selves and self-doubt: A poverty of desired possibility. *Social Psychological and Personality Science,* 2(2), 190-198.

Chandler, J. (2010). Women and men as managers: The importance of disappointment. *Gender, Work and Organization,* 17(5), 590-611.

Chen, S.A. (2016). *Film review. Hidden Figures.* Common Sense Media. Retrieved from https://www.commonsensemedia.org/movie-reviews/hidden-figures.

Cerel, J., Fristad, M.A., Verducci, J., Weller, R.A., Weller, E.B. (2006). Childhood bereavement: Psychopathology in the 2 years postparental death. *Journal of American Academy Child and Adolescent Psychiatry,* 45(6), 681-690.

Clark, I.A., Holmes, E.A., Woolrich, M.W. & Mackay, C.E. (2016). Intrusive memories to traumatic footage: the neural basis of their encoding and involuntary recall (2016). *Psychological Medicine,* 46, 505-518.

"cognitive function". (n.d.) *Mosby's Medical Dictionary, 8th edition.* (2009). October 9, 2017.

https://medical-dictionary.thefreedictionary.com/cognitive+function.

Connolly, T. & Zeelenberg, M. (2002). Regret in decision making. *American Psychological Society,* 11(6), 212-216.

Cordner, C. (2016). Unconditional love? *Cogent Arts & Humanities,* 3, p. 1-12.

Dalton, P.S., Gonzalez Jimenez, V.H. & Noussair, C.H. (2017). Exposure to poverty and productivity. *PloS One,* 12(1), 1-19.

Dalton, P.S., Ghosal, S., Mani, A. (2014). Poverty and aspirations failure. *The Economic Journal,* 165-188.

Davis, C.G., Nolen-Hoeksema, S., & Larson, J. (1998). Making sense of loss and benefiting from the experience: Two construals of meaning. *Journal of Personality and Social Psychology,* 75(2), 561-574.

Debruge, P. (2016). *Film review: Hidden Figures.* Retrieved from http://variety.com/2016/film/reviews/hidden-figures-review 1201936516/.

DeMarco, D. (2015). Too late for regret. *Human Life Review,* 41(4), 55-60.

Dennis, M.R., Ridder, K., & Dennis Kunkel, A. (2006). Grief, glory, and political capital in the capitol: Presidents eulogizing presidents. *Death Studies,* 30, 325-349.

Dictionary, n.d. (2018, January 15). Agape. *Dictionary.com.* Retrieved from http://www.dictionary.com/browse/agape.

Dost, A. & Yagmurlu, B. (2008). Are constructiveness and destructiveness essential features of guilt and shame feelings respectively? *Journal for the Theory of Social Behaviour,* 38(2), 109-129.

Dowdney, L. (2000). Annotation: Childhood bereavement following parental death. *Journal of Child Psychology and Psychiatry,* 41(7), 819-830.

Ellison, R. (1952). *Invisible Man.* New York, NY: Random House.

Elshtain, J.B. (2013). On Loyalty: A Monthly Journal of Religion and Public Life. *A Monthly Journal*, 235, 27-31.

Fernandez-Alcantara, M., Perez-Garcia, M., Perez-Marfil, N., Catena-Martinez, A. Hueso-Montoro, C. & Cruz-Quintana, F. (2016). Assessment of different components of executive function in grief. *Psicothema*, 28(3), 260-265.

Feys, M., Anseel, F. & Wille, B. (2012). Responses to co-worker receiving recognition at work. *Journal of Managerial Psychology,* 28(5), 492-510.

Freud, S. (1920), (1961). *Beyond the pleasure principle. Standard Edition.* W.W. Norton & Company, Inc.

Fromm, E. (1956). *The art of loving.* New York, NY, USA: Harper & Row.

Gabbard, G. (2005). *Psychodynamic Psychiatry in Clinical Practice. Fourth Edition.* Washington, D.C. American Psychiatric Publishing, Inc.

Gaiman, N. (2008). *The Graveyard Book.* New York, NY: HarperCollins Publishers.

Gausel, N., Vignoles, V.L. & Leach, C.W. (2016). Resolving the paradox of shame: Differentiating among specific appraisal-feeling combinations explains pro-social and self-defensive motivation. *Motivation and Emotion*, 40, 118-139.

Getter, A. (2012). Unconditional love. *Journal of Palliative Medicine,* 15(9), 1040.

Gibaldi, C.P. (2013). The changing trends of retirement: Baby boomers leading the change. *Review of Business,* 34(1), 50-57.

Gray, L.B., Weller, R.A., Fristad, M., Weller, E.B. (2011). Depression in children and Adolescents who months after the death of a parent. *Journal of Affective Disorders,* 135, 277-283.

Greenberg, L., Warwar, S., & Malcolm, W. (2010). Emotion-focused couples therapy and the facilitation of forgiveness. *Journal of Marital and Family Therapy,* 36(1), 28-42.

Greenberg, J. (2015). Disappointment: Something in the nature of analysis. *JAPA,* 63(6), 1215-1223.

Grolleau, G., Mzoughi, M. & Pekovic, S. (2015). Work recognition and labor productivity: Evidence from french data. *Managerial and Decision Economics,* 36, 508-516.

Grotevant, H. D., Dunbar, N., Kohler, J.K. & Lash Esau, A.M. (2000). Adoptive Identity: How contexts within and beyond the family shape developmental pathways. *Family Relations,* 49(4), 379-387.

Guzman, A.B. de, Llantino, M.L.S., See, V.C.L., Villaneuva, R.F.P., Jung, Y. (2008). Horizon, not boundaries, are the language of retirement: Sense of fulfillment, fears, and life trajectories of faculty extendees in the Philippines. *Educational Gerontology,* 34, 749-762.

Harvard Medical Health Letter (2011). *Beyond the five stages of grief.* Retrieved from www.health.harvard.edu.

Herman, J. (1992). *Trauma and Recovery. The Aftermath of Violence-From Domestic Abuse to Political Terror.* New York, NY. BasicBooks.

Hermann, A.D., Leonardelli, G, J. & Arkin, R.M. (2002). Self-doubt and self-esteem: A threat from within. *Personality and Social Psychology Bulletin,* 28(3), 395-408.

Hill, T.E. (2016). Conscientious conviction and conscience. *Criminal Law and Philosophy,* 10, 677-692.

Hjemdal, O. (2007). Measuring protective factors: the development of two resilience scales in Norway. *Child and Adolescent Psychiatric Clinics of North America,* 16, 303-321.

Howe, D & Feast, J. (2001). The long-term outcome of reunions between adult adopted people and their birth mothers. *The British Journal of Social Work,* 31(3), 351-368.

Inzlicht, M., McGregor, I, Hirsh, J.B. & Nash, K. (2009). Neural markers of religious conviction. *Psychological Science,* 20(3), 385-392.

Ives, J. (2008). Does a belief in God lead to moral cowardice? The difference between courage of moral conviction and acquisition. *Think,* 7, 57-89.

James, W. (1950). *The principles of psychology* (Vol.1). New York, NY, USA: Dover. (Original work published 1890).

Joel, S. MacDonald, G. & Plaks, J.E. (2012). Attachment anxiety uniquely predicts regret proneness in close relationship contexts. *Social Psychology and Personality Science,* 3(3), 348-355.

Johnson, S.M., Makinen, J.A., & Millikin, J.W. (2001). Attachment injuries in couples relationships: A new perspective on impasses in couples therapy. *Journal of Marital and Family Therapy,* 27(2), 145-155.

Jones, K. (2017). Regret and affirmation. Journal of Applied Philosophy, 34(3), 414-419.

Joseph, Ph.D., S. (2012, October 7). *Unconditional positive regard. If you think it's about smiling and nodding you are doing it wrong. Psychology Today.* https://www.psychologytoday.com/us/blog/what-doesnt-kill

us/201210/unconditional-positive-regard.

Kalb, C. (2017). Genius. National Geographic, May, p. 30-55.

Keyes, K.M., Pratt, C., Galea, S., McLaughlin, K.A., Koenen, K.C., Shear, M.K. (2014). The burden of loss: Unexpected death of a loved one and psychiatric disorders across the life course in a national study. *American Journal of Psychiatry,* 171, 864-871.

Kroll, B. (2004). Living with an elephant: Growing up with parental substance misuse. *Child and Family Social Work,* 9, 129-140.

Kristensen, P., Weisaeth, L., Heir, T. (2012). Bereavement and mental health after sudden and violent losses: a review. *Psychiatry,* 75(1), 76-97.

Kubler-Ross, E. (1969). *On Death and Dying.* New York. Scribner.

LaFreniere, L. & Cain, A. (2015). Parentally bereaved children and adolescents: The question of peer support. *Journal of Death and Dying,* 71(3), 245-271.

Laub, D., Lee, S. (2002). Thanatos and massive psychic trauma: The impact of the death instinct on knowing, remembering and forgetting. *Journal of American Psychoanalytic Association,* 51, 433-464.

Lichtenthal, W.G., Currier, J.M., Neimeyer, R.A., & Keesee, N.J. (2010). Sense and significance: A mixed methods examination of meaning making after the loss of one's child. *Journal of Clinical Psychology,* 66(7), 791-812.

Lifton, B.J. (2010). Ghosts in the Adopted Family. *Psychoanalytic Inquiry,* 30, 71-79.

Lillyman, M.A., S. (2007). Fear of social isolation: Results of a survey of older adults in Gloucestershire. *Nursing Older People,* 19(10), 26-28.

Lind, J. (2011). Roots, origins and backgrounds: An analysis of their meaning in the creation of adoptive families in Sweden. *Childhood,* 19(1), 115-128.

Lindgren, C. & Zetterqvist Nelson, K. (2014). Here and now-there and then: Narrative time and space in intercountry adoptees' stories about background, origin and roots. *Qualitative Social Work,* 13(4), 539-554.

Liu, E. & Roloff, M.E. (2016). Regret for complaint withholding. *Communication Quarterly,* 64(1), 72-92.

Lockwood, P. & Kunda, Z. (1997). Superstars and me: Predicting the impact of role models on the self. *Journal of Personality and Social Psychology,* 73(1), 91-103.

Long, R.J. & Shields, J.L. (2010). "From pay to praise? Non-cash employee recognition in Canadian and Australian firms". *The International Journal of Human Resource Management,* 21(8), 1145-1172.

Luchies, L.B., Finkel, E.J., McNulty, J.K., & Kumashiro, M. (2010). The doormat effect: When forgiving erodes self-respect and self-concept clarity. *Journal of Personality and Social Psychology,* 98(5), 734-749.

Luttrell, A., Petty, R.E., Brinol, P. & Wagner, B.C., (2016). Making it moral: Merely labeling an attitude as moral increases its strength. *Journal of Experimental Social Psychology,* 65, 82-93.

MacDonald, M. & McSherry, D. (2011). Open adoption. Adoptive parents' experiences of birth family contact and talking to their child about adoption. *Adoption & Fostering,* 35(3), 4-16.

Maciejewski, P.K., Maercker, A., Bolen, P.A., Prigerson, H.G. (2016). "Prolonged grief disorder" and "persistent complex bereavement disorder", but not complicated grief', "are one and the same diagnostic entity: An analysis of data from the Yale bereavement study. *World Psychiatry,* 15(3), 266-275.

Madsen, M. & Abell, N. (2010). Trauma resilience scale: validation of protective factors associated with adaptation following violence. *Research on Social Work Practice,* 20(2) 223-233.

Mammen, S., Dolan, E., Seiling, S.B., (2015). Explaining the poverty dynamics of rural families using an economic well-being continuum. *Journal of Family Economics Issues,* 36, 434-450.

Mani, A., Mullainathan, S., Shafir, E. & Zhao, J. (2017). Poverty impedes cognitive function. *Science,* 341(6149), p. 976-980.

Marcatto, F. & Ferrante, D. (2008). The regret and disappointment scale: An instrument for assessing regret and disappointment in decision making. *Judgment and Decision Making,* 3(1), 87-99.

March, K. (1995). Perception of adoption as social stigma: Motivation for search and reunion. *Journal of Marriage and Family,* 57(3), 653-660.

Marquez, M.I. (2014). The development of the self through the "gift of the self" or the mutual recognition. *Journal of Perspectives of Economic Political and Social Integration,* 19(1), 143-153.

Masterson, A. (2012). Retrospective reports of the lived school experience of adolescents after the death of a parent. *The Journal of School Nursing,* 29(5), 370-377.

McNeish, D. (2013). Grief is a circular staircase: The use and limits of models of grief on the pastoral care of the bereaved. *Practical Theology,* 6(2), 190-203.

McWilliams, N. (2011). *Psychoanalytic Diagnosis, Second Edition.* New York, NY. Guilford Press, p. 139.

Merriam-Webster, n.d. (2017). Bereavement. *Merriam-Webster.com.* Retrieved from https://www.merriam-webster.com/dictionary/bereavement.

Merriam-Webster, n.d. (2017). Defense Mechanism. *Merriam-Webster.com.* Retrieved from https://www.merriamwebster.com/dictionary/defensemechanism.

Merriam-Webster, n.d. (2017). Loyal. *Merriam-Webster.com.* Retrieved from https://www.merriam-webster.com/dictionary/loyal.

Merriam-Webster, n.d. (2017). Poverty. *Merriam-Webster.com.* Retrieved from https://www.merriam-webster.com/dictionary/poverty.

Merriam-Webster, n.d. (2017). Resilience. *Merriam-Webster.com.* Retrieved from https://www.merriam-webster.com/dictionary/resilience.

Merriam-Webster, n.d. (2017, December 28). Self-doubt. *Merriam-Webster.com.* Retrieved from https://www.merriam-webster.com/dictionary/self-doubt.

Merriam-Webster, n.d. (2017). Withholding. *Merriam-Webster.com.* Retrieved from https://www.merriam-webster.com/dictionary/withholding.

Mullin, A. (2006). Parents and Children: An alternative to selfless and unconditional love. *Hypatia,* 21(1), p. 181-200.

Munoz-Darde, V. (2016). Puzzles of regret. *Philosophy and Phenomenological Research,* XCII (3), 778-784.

Neria, Y. & Litz, B. T. (2003). Bereavement by traumatic means: The complex synergy of trauma and grief. *Journal of Loss and Trauma,* 9, 73-87.

Nguyen, S., Tirrito, T.S., Barkey, W.M. (2014). Fear as a predictor of life satisfaction in retirement in Canada. Educational Gerontology, 40, 102-122.

O'Donohue, J. (1997). *Anam Cara: A Book on Celtic Wisdom.* New York, NY: HarperCollins Publishers, Inc.

Oleson, K.C., Poehlmann, K. M., Yost, J. H., Lynch, M.E. & Arkin, R.M. 2000). Subjective overachievement: Individual differences in self-doubt and concern with performance. *Journal of Personality,* 68(3), 491-524.

O'Rourke, M. (2010, February 1). Good grief. Is there a better way to be bereaved? *The New Yorker.*

Palahniuk, C. (1999). *Invisible Monsters.* New York, NY: W.W. Norton & Company, Inc.

Palomar Lever, J., Lanzagorta Piñol, N., Hernández Uralde, J. (2005). Poverty, psychological resources and subjective well-being. *Social Indicators Research,* 73(3), 375-408.

Paris, R., Herriott, A., Holt, M. & Gould, K. (2015). Differential responsiveness to parenting intervention for mothers in substance abuse treatment. *Child Abuse and Neglect,* 50, 206-217.

Peer, J.W. & McAuslan, P. (2016). Self-doubt during emerging adulthood: The conditional mediating influence of mindfulness. *Emerging Adulthood,* 4(3), 176-185.

Pianalto, M. (2011). Moral conviction. *Journal of Applied Philosophy,* 28(4), 381-395.

Rachman, S. (2010). Betrayal: A psychological analysis. *Behaviour Research and Therapy,* 48, 304-311.

Regan, P.C. (2016). Loving unconditionally: Demographic correlates of the agapic love style. *Interpersona,* 10(1), 28-35.

Reifman, A., Arnett, J.J. & Colwell, M.J. (2007). Emerging Adulthood: Theory, Assessment and Application. *Journal of Youth Development,* 2(1), 1-12.

Reifman, A. & Grahe, J.E. (2016). Introduction to the special issue of emerging adulthood. *Emerging Adulthood,* 4(3), 135-141.

Reinoso, M., Juffer, F. & Tieman, W. (2013). Children's and parents' thoughts and feelings about adoption, birth culture identity and discrimination in families with internationally adopted children. *Child and Family Social Work,* 18, 264-274.

Robinaugh, D.J., LeBlanc, N.J., Vuletich, H.A. & McNally, R.J. (2014). Network Analysis of Persistent Complex Bereavement Disorder in Conjugally Bereaved Adults. *Journal of Abnormal Psychology,* 123(3), 510-522.

Roese, N.J. & Summerville, A. (2005). What we regret most….and why. *Personality and Social Psychology Bulletin,* 31(9), 1273-1285.

Rostilla, M., Berg, L., Arat, A., Vinnerijung, B., Hjern, A. (2016). Parental death in childhood and self-inflected injuries in young adults-a national cohort study from Sweden. *European Child & Adolescent Psychiatry,* 25, 1103-1111.

Sakamoto, A., Rarick, J., Woo, H., Wang, S.X. (2014). What underlies the Great Gatsby Curve? Psychological micro-foundations of the "vicious circle" of poverty. *Mind & Society,* 13, 195-211.

Sartorius, N. (2007). Stigma and mental health. *The Lancet, 370,* 810-811.

Scheff, T.J. (2000). Shame and the social bond: A sociological theory. *Sociological Theory,* 18(1), 84-99.

Schilbach, F., Schofield, H., & Mullainathan, S. (2016). The psychological lives of the poor. *American Economic Review: Papers & Proceedings,* 106(5), 435-440.

Schimmell, N. (2008). A humanistic approach to caring for street children: The importance of emotionally intimate and supportive relationships for the successful rehabilitation of street children. *Vulnerable Children and Youth Studies*, 3(3), 214-220.

Sebastian, C., Burnett, S. & Blakemore, S-J. (2008). Development of the self-concept during adolescence. *Trends in Cognitive Science,* 12(22), 441-446.

Seeman, N. (2015). Use data to challenge mental-health stigma. *Nature,* 528, 309.

Shear, M.K., Simon, N., Wall, M., Zisook, S., Neimeyer, R.m Duan, N., Reynolds, C., Lebowitz, B., Sung, S., Ghesquiere, A., Gorscak, B., Clayton, P., Ito, M., Nakajima, S., Konishi, T., Melhem, N., Meert, K., Schiff, M., O'Connor, M.F., First, M., Sareen, J., Bolton, J., Skritskaya, N., Mancini, A., Keshaviah, A. (2011). Complicated grief and related bereavement issues for DSM-5. *Depression and Anxiety.* 28, 103-117.

Shenk, M.K. & Scelza, B.A. (2012). Paternal investment and status-related child outcomes: Timing of father's death affects offspring success. Journal of Biosocial Science, 44, 549-569.

Simon, N.M. (2013). Treating complicated grief. *JAMA,* 310(4), 416-423.

Skitka, L.J. & Scott Morgan, G. (2014). The social and political implications of moral conviction. *Advances in Political Psychology,* 35(1), 95-110.

Skitka, L.J. & Mullen, E. (2002). The dark side of moral conviction. *Analyses of Social Issues and Public Policy,* 35-41.

Skitka, L.J. & Wisneski, D.C. (2011). Moral conviction and emotion. *Emotion Review,* 3(3), 328-330.

Smit, C. (2015). Theories and models of grief: Applications to professional practice. *Whitireia Nursing and Health Journal,* 322, 33-37.

Smith, J.M. & Estefan, A. (2014). Families parenting adolescents with substance abuse-Recovering the mother's voice: A narrative literature review. *Journal of Family Nursing,* 20(4), 415-441.

Snaman, J.M., Kaye, E.C., Torres, C., Gibson, D. & Baker, J.N. (2016). Parental grief following the death of a child from cancer: The ongoing odyssey. *Pediatric Blood Cancer,* 63, 1594-1602.

Sprecher, S. & Fehr, B. (2005). Compassionate love for close others and humanity. *Journal of Social and Personal Relationships,* 22(5), 629-651.

Stikkelbroek, Y., Prinzie, P., de Graf, R., ten Have, M., Cuijpers, P. (2012). Parental death during childhood and psychopathology in adulthood. *Psychiatry Research,* 198, 516-520.

Stroebe, M. & Schut, H. (2010). The dual process model of coping with bereavement: A decade on\*. *Omega,* 61(4), 273-289.

Stroebe, M., Stroebe, W., Schut, H., Boerner, K. (2017). Grief is not a disease but bereavement merits medical awareness. *The Lancet,* 389, 347-349.

Suchy, Y. (2009). Executive functioning: Overview, assessment and research issues for non- neuropsychologists. *Annals Behavioral Medicine,* 37, 106-116.

Ungar, M. (2013). Resilience, trauma, context and culture. *Trauma, Violence, & Abuse,* 14(3) 255-266.

Tangney, J.P., Stuewig, J., & Martinez, A.G. (2014). Two faces of shame: The roles of shame and guilt in predicting recidivism. Psychological Science, 25(3), 799-805.

Thieleman, K. & Cacciatrore, J. (2014). When a child dies: A critical analysis of grief-related controversies in DSM-5. *Research on Social Work Practice,* 24(1), 114-122.

US Department of Health and Human Services (2017). http://www.ncsl.org/research/health/2014-federal-poverty-levelstandards.aspx#1.

Van Der Kolk, B. M.D. (2014). *The body keeps the score. Brain, mind and body in the healing of trauma.* New York, NY: Penguin Books.

Vega, P., Soledad Rivera, M. & Gonzalez, R. (2014). When grief turns into love: Understanding the experience of parents who have revived after losing a child due to cancer. *Journal of Pediatric Oncology Nursing,* 31(3), 166-176.

Verducci, S. (2014). Self-doubt: One moral of the story. *Studies in Philosophy and Education,* 33, 609-620.

Verwoerd, J., Wessel, I., de Jong, P.J., Nieuwenhuis, M.M.W., Huntjens, R.J.C. (2011). Pre-stressor interference control and intrusive memories. *Cognitive Therapy Research,* 35, 161-170.

Walt Disney Quotes. (n.d.). BrainyQuotes.com.

https://www.brainyquote.com/quotes/walt_disney_163027

Wang, L.K., Ponte, I.C. & Weber Ollen, E. (2015). Letting her go: Western adoptive families' search and reunion with Chinese birth parents. *Adoption Quarterly,* 18, 45-66.

Wijngaards-De Meij, L., Stroebe, M., Schut, H., Stroebe, W., Van den Bout, J., Van der Heijden, P., Dijkstra, I. (2005). Couples at risk following the death of their child: Predictors of grief versus depression. *Journal of Consulting and Clinical Psychology,* 73, 617-623.

Winter, K. & Cohen, C. (2005). Identity issues for looked after children with no knowledge of their origins. Implications for research and practice. *Adoption & Fostering,* 29(2), 44-52.

Wright, J.C., Cullum, J. & Schwab, N. (2008). The cognitive and affective dimensions of moral conviction: Implications for attitudinal and behavioral measures of interpersonal tolerance. *Personality and Social Psychology Bulletin,* 34(11), 1461-1476.

Wrobel, G.M., Grotevant, H.D., Samek, D.R. & Von Korff, L. (2013). Adoptees' curiosity and information-seeking about birth parents in emerging adulthood: Context, motivation and behavior. *International Journal of Behavioral Development,* 37(5), 441-450.

Wubben, M.J.J., De Cremer, D., van Dijk, E. (2009). How emotion communication guides reciprocity: Establishing cooperation through disappointment and anger. *Journal of Experimental Social Psychology,* 45, 987-990.

Zhao, Q. & Wichman, A. (2015). Incremental belief about ability ameliorate self-doubt effects. *SAGE,* 1-10.

Xu, Y., Herman, H., Tsutsumi, A., Fisher, J. (2012). Psychological and social consequences of losing a child in a natural or human-made disaster: A review of the evidence. *Asia-Pacific Psychiatry,* 5(4), 237-248.

## *ABOUT THE AUTHOR*

Katherine Marshall Woods, Psy.D. is a licensed clinical psychologist providing psychotherapy and psychological assessments in Washington, DC. She earned her Bachelor of Arts and doctoral degrees from The George Washington University. Dr. Marshall Woods has served as a certified school psychologist within DC Public Schools as well as provided psychotherapy services to active military personnel in Doha, Qatar.

Today, Dr. Marshall Woods is in private practice with Psychological Group of Washington, is a member of the core faculty at The George Washington University—where she teaches psychological assessments and trauma—and is the Assistant Director of Psychology at Psychiatric Institute of Washington. She is also a faculty member of the Washington School of Psychiatry, teaching clinical supervision skills for mental health professionals. Dr. Marshall Woods has over a decade of experience supervising clinical work and provides services with the Chinese American Psychoanalytic Alliance, supervising mental health practitioners providing services in China. Further, she holds interest in the intersection between psychology and film, where she has contributed blogs for The Huffington Post, the former American Psychological Association's PsycCRITIQUES, and currently blogs with Thrive Global and Medium within this arena. Lastly, Dr. Marshall Woods has lent her expertise to a number of media outlets, such as News Channel 8, NPR, The Huffington Post, and The Daily Drum; and works with actors, screenwriters, producers, and directors on theme and character development and set accuracy.

## BEST PSYCHOLOGY IN FILM

www.ingramcontent.com/pod-product-compliance
Lightning Source LLC
Chambersburg PA
CBHW071346290426
44108CB00014B/1456